My Sister Marilyn

My Sister Marilyn

A MEMOIR OF MARILYN MONROE

BERNIECE BAKER MIRACLE and **MONA RAE MIRACLE**

iUniverse, Inc.
Bloomington

My Sister Marilyn
A memoir of Marilyn Monroe

iUniverse books may be ordered through booksellers or by contacting:

iUniverse
1663 Liberty Drive
Bloomington, IN 47403
www.iuniverse.com
1-800-Authors (1-800-288-4677)

ISBN: 978-1-4759-6808-8 (sc)
ISBN: 978-1-4759-6809-5 (ebk)

Printed in the United States of America

iUniverse rev. date: 12/27/2012

To Violet Cameron, Edna Gillett, and Mavis Hewett, who contributed specialized counsel and encouragement; to friends whose enthusiasm was contagious; to the Writers' Workshop of Asheville who brought us together with our editor; to the Marilyn fans whose adoration of her was boundless; and to the elves at Algonquin who get birthday presents ready on time, our sincere thanks.

For Paris

Contents

A Note from the Authors

Many writers approached my mother Berniece and offered to help tell her story but, after all that had been written about Marilyn, she didn't trust their motives and couldn't know whether the hours she devoted to the project would bring only more grief.

When I began cultivating my desire to be a writer, she asked me for assistance. I was reluctant at first. I had developed my career without reference to Marilyn; in fact, once I finished school and left Florida, I never told anyone about my connection to our famous relative. I wanted to be judged on my own merits, so I wasn't eager to link my career to Marilyn. But Mother wanted strongly to set the record straight, so I came to see my work on this book as a gift to her.

When she came to stay at my house to work on the book, we sat down with a tape recorder and notepad, ready to call up everything in our memory. On the very first day of work, we got a call telling us my grandmother, Mamita, had disappeared. Mother had to return home as police detectives scoured several states trying to locate her. We continued to work around several such family crises.

Once I began to piece together our memories on paper, I challenged myself to shape the material into a work that would mirror Marilyn's multifaceted personality. From the start, I constructed the book by weaving narrative and reflection with dramatization of our most vivid memories.

Speaking the truth about the Marilyn we knew after so many years of tabloid coverage was like David facing Goliath. We expected a long search for a publisher who wouldn't press us to inject false sensationalism into the book, but we became discouraged nonetheless and set the project aside for several years.

One day in the spring of 1993, I had been gazing out a rain streaked window, thinking of our book. I spoke aloud, though no one was present, as I asked, "What should we do? Would Marilyn want us to go ahead?" As if in answer, a rainbow appeared, arching between two apple trees right in my back yard.

So as a birthday present, I took Mother to a workshop on getting published, given by an editor from Algonquin Books of Chapel Hill. The editor was Lisa Poteet, who, with the enthusiasm of a true Marilyn scholar, has seen to it that this book appeared for Marilyn's own next birthday.

Mona Rae Miracle

My Sister Marilyn tells the story of my sister and me. We share the same mother, who early in our lives was diagnosed as mentally ill. We grew up feeling abandoned and, though both of us were told we were pretty and talented, we still needed courage and strength. We got that from each other.

Marilyn's star was already rising when she was only twenty. Her privacy was so important to her, though preserving it was always an unattainable goal because the press chased after every tidbit of news about her. When Jim Dougherty's sister Billie talked to the press, Marilyn saw her as disloyal, though the story didn't paint her in an unfavorable light. At times I was tempted to correct some of the misperceptions about Marilyn and her background, but I didn't want Marilyn to lose trust in me. I wanted to be a source of love and support for her.

When Marilyn's sorrow was limelighted in the papers as her marriage to Joe DiMaggio failed, I began to wonder if a real private life would ever be possible for Marilyn in the glare of such media interest. I think her desire for privacy was a big part of why she gave out fake stories about her background through her public relations people. She thought that she could preserve my normal life and my family's and that she could protect our mother's privacy by giving false leads to the press.

When Marilyn died, I was devastated. I don't think I have been quite the same since. Over the years I have read too many accounts of her life and ours so filled with errors that they present a woman I hardly recognize. Some things that have been published about Marilyn's life are such fabrications that further comment would be less than worthy. But of all the distortions that have circulated since her death, I have always wanted most keenly to erase the myth that Marilyn had no family to love her.

A friend of mine told me, "Berniece, your silence creates a void that leaves room for these distortions and errors to flourish. If you don't tell your story, how will fans ever know what your sister was really like?"

So I decided to break my silence. I wanted Marilyn's fans to see the human Marilyn behind the public image and to understand the complicated relationship she and I had with our mother. I wanted to offer a book that shows Marilyn as I knew her for those who admired Marilyn's talent and fortitude during her lifetime and for those who remain loyal fans today.

These are our memories of Marilyn, presented with love.

Berniece Baker Miracle

Part One

"You Have a Sister . . ."

Chapter One

I remember waiting at the train station in Detroit for Marilyn to appear that first time—of course, then she was still Norma Jeane. We had been writing to each other over the years and had exchanged pictures, but we had never met face to face. She'd told me she'd be wearing a cobalt blue suit and a hat with a heart shaped brim, but I worried that I wouldn't recognize her when she stepped off the train.

There was no missing her! She stood out immediately from all the rest of the passengers, so tall and pretty and fresh. We were excited to finally meet, and we couldn't stop staring at each other. We had the same dark blond hair with a widow's peak, the same mouth, but our eyes were different—mine are brown and Norma Jeane's were blue like our mother's. I was so happy to have a sister. And so proud.

But when I was growing up I didn't even know if my mother was still alive. And I didn't find out about Norma Jeane until she was twelve and I was nineteen.

Kentucky, 1923

Four-year old Berniece Baker clutches the cold steel rail of the bridge. The wind flails strands of her blond hair against her face like tiny whips. She squints her eyelids against the wind and watches the two women nearby. One is her stepmother. One is her mother by blood.

The stepmother, bony and dark haired, leans with the stiffness of middle age. The wind blows her straight-cut bangs away from her forehead, revealing deep frown lines. At twenty-three, the other woman has the unlined face of a girl. The animation of her petite body matches the erratic energy of the wind. The child watches this young flaxen-haired stranger gesture angrily and turn on her heel. Her shoulders grow smaller and disappear below the crest of the bridge.

The gaunt older woman turns and stoops, folding her arms about the child for a long moment. She takes the child's hand, and together they tread across the rough planks of the bridge, their shoes making faint hollow taps, the taps carried away by the wind.

Gladys Monroe Baker, the young fair-haired stranger, disappears just as mysteriously as she had appeared in the lives of her ex-husband Jasper Baker, her daughter Berniece, her son Jackie, and Jasper's wife, Maggie. As time passes, year after year without a word, the family will wonder if she is still alive. But Gladys's incredible energy and anger simply propel her from Kentucky back to California with a determination to resume her life there anew.

At the film lab where she works, Gladys meets a coworker with whom she has much in common. Grace Atchinson McKee, age twenty-nine, is also divorced, also a film cutter. The two become best friends and roommates. Their arrangement lasts until Gladys, at the urging of her mother, accepts the proposal of Edward Mortensen. They are married on October 11, 1924. On the marriage certificate, Edward lists his name as Martin E. Mortensen; his age as twenty-seven; his occupation, meter-man; his birthplace, California; his marital status, divorced. Gladys lists her age as twenty-two, although she is actually twenty-four.

On May 27, 1926, Gladys's mother, Della (widowed in 1909 when Gladys's father, Otis Elmer Monroe died, and now married to Charles Grainger), dispatches a picture postcard to Kentucky from Borneo, where her engineer husband is on assignment. Addressing that card to Berniece, and evidently unaware that Gladys had broken contact with the child, Della writes:

> Dear Little Berniece, This is the kind of big snakes they have here. They are big enough they could swallow you & Jackie and so could the alligators. They have lots of fun here hunting them. This is your mother's birthday. Do you and Jackie ever write to her, write to me. Your Grand Mother Mrs. Chas. Grainger.

Five days later on June 1, Gladys gives birth to her second daughter, Norma Jeane Mortenson. (Though Gladys's husband's name appears as "Mortensen" on their marriage certificate, on Norma Jeane's birth certificate the spelling has changed slightly.) On the birth certificate, Gladys indicates that this is her third child but falsely states that it is the only living one. "Mortenson's" address is listed as unknown, his occupation as that of baker. He has left Gladys before the birth and disappeared.

Gladys is completely without means. Norma Jeane was born in a charity ward, and Gladys must find someone to care for her infant daughter so that she can return to work. Della's neighbors in nearby Hawthorne, California, agree to board Norma Jeane. Gladys pays Albert Wayne Bolender and his wife Ida twenty-five dollars a month.

Gladys visits Norma Jeane on weekends and takes her for outings, including sleepovers at her apartment in Los Angeles. When Della returns to Hawthorne, ill with malaria, often delirious, suffering fevers and delusions, she is unable to care for Norma Jeane. So the boarding arrangement continues. Norma Jeane is fourteen months old when Della dies at age fifty-one in August 1927. Gladys handles the details and expenses of Della's funeral, placing Della's grave alongside that of her first husband.

Norma Jeane begins kindergarten at Washington Avenue School in Hawthorne. Her closest companion is Lester, a foster child of the Bolenders, whom they eventually adopt. Norma Jeane is healthy, strong, athletic, and keeps pace with Lester in their backyard contests. As she builds memories, she banks the fond affection of the Bolenders, the delight she feels wearing the fancy dresses that Ida sews for her, and a sense of accomplishment as she takes piano lessons. Her lifelong love of animals begins with her mutt Tippy. She suffers terrible grief when Tippy is shot by a neighbor.

In the fall of 1933, Gladys realizes a dream she has worked toward with endless overtime hours. After scrimping for seven years, she has finally saved enough money for a down payment on a home for herself and Norma Jeane, a two-story house near the Hollywood Bowl. To help meet expenses, she rents rooms to a British couple and their grown daughter, all movie stand-ins.

5

Norma Jeane, who is seven, now transfers to Selma Avenue School. Gladys's special gift to Norma Jeane is a piano to call her very own, a black Franklin grand, once owned by Fredric March.

Gladys's friend Grace McKee advises Gladys not to buy the house because their future at the film lab is insecure. And Grace's forebodings are borne out. Recent years have been stressful for Gladys—divorce, desertion, the death of her mother, separation from two of her children, the frustration of dead end dating, the toll of working overtime, and now a strike at her company just when she has taken on the huge financial obligation of a home. The accumulated stress results in a breakdown.

Gladys must be hospitalized and is diagnosed as suffering from paranoid schizophrenia. Grace takes responsibility for handling Gladys's affairs, becoming guardian for both Gladys and Norma Jeane. Grace's sister and brother-in-law, Enid and Sam Knebelkamp, and her Aunt Ana Lower help care for Norma Jeane. Gladys's house is sold and the furniture auctioned off, but Ana Lower buys Norma Jeane's piano to hold in safekeeping for her.

Grace is responsible for handling Gladys's company insurance money, and, as Gladys's illness continues beyond the term of coverage, Grace must transfer her from the hospital to a state institution. It becomes apparent that Gladys is not going to recover in the near future, making it necessary for Grace to place Norma Jeane in the Los Angeles County Children's Home. Grace promised to honor Gladys's plea that Norma Jeane neither be adopted nor taken out of the state of California.

When nine-year old Norma Jeane moves to the children's home on September 13, 1935, she must once again transfer to a new school, this time Vine Elementary. Norma Jeane remains at the children's home until Grace's circumstances improve. She leaves on June 26, 1937, at the age of eleven, to live in the home of "Aunt" Grace and her new husband Erwin C. Goddard. "Doc" Goddard is an engineer and amateur inventor. He is divorced, with custody of his three young children. Norma Jeane's "siblings" now include Doc's daughter Bebe, age nine; son "Fritz" (John), age seven; and daughter Josephine, age five. A family of Persian cats and a spaniel round out the large, active household. Norma Jeane attends Sawtelle Elementary, and then Emerson Junior High School.

The echo of staccato, syncopated taps fills the cavernous three-story stairwell. Blond-haired sixteen-year old Berniece Baker clatters down the steps of Pineville High School in Kentucky, improvising a tap dance. Below, her audience leaps and shrieks. Niobe Miracle and two other friends are enthusiastic and raucous.

Berniece lands in a split at the bottom of the stairs. The girls clap wildly. Berniece grins, breathless. They haul her up, laughing, and bounce together through the open back doors, not really worried that the principal may be striding down the corridor to investigate this explosion of noise a half hour after school has been dismissed. The principal has heard this noise before. In the spring, she will smile to find the thundering energy transformed into a song-and-dance routine performed to the popular tune "College Rhythm."

I won First Prize in the talent show that year. I wore black slacks and a white satin blouse, copied from a movie I had seen. I didn't stick to the steps I had been rehearsing, but it was pretty good, and the audience loved it. I was thrilled with my five dollars prize money. I thought it was a fortune! So did everybody else in 1935.

7

"College Rhythm" tinkles out of radios from coast to coast. Three thousand miles away another slim blond girl, this one just eleven years old but equally interested in music and mirrors, is groping through some confusing times after her move from an orphanage in Los Angeles to the home of her mother's best friend Grace and Grace's new husband. Norma Jeane finds that listening to music lifts her spirits. Hearing tunes spun by the disc jockeys over and over again gives a pattern to her days, a pleasant order and familiarity.

She wonders if she will be allowed to resume the piano lessons that stopped abruptly when her mother became ill. It would be nice to get beyond the keyboard exercise books and play something like the popular tunes on the radio. Like "College Rhythm."

Going to the movies on Saturdays becomes Norma Jeane's favorite pastime, and, as she enters adolescence, fantasy life fills her private moments. She experiments with makeup for hours, and she acts out roles she has seen in films. Yet she has more success at school with athletics than with acting. Norma Jeane wins a track medal but is not cast in a play, although she does perform in a talent show.

Paris Miracle and Berniece escape the monotony of school one rainy day, squeezing into the backseat with a carful of noontime hamburger stand seekers. "I have a ring for you," whispers Paris. A tiny blue box materializes. Paris opens it, slips out a solitaire, and twists it onto Berniece's finger. Berniece's reply is lost among the screams of the car's teenagers, as the driver makes a 360 degree skid on the rain-slick mountain road.

Back at school, Paris's sister Niobe attempts to scratch the window of their home economics classroom to discover if Berniece's ring is a genuine diamond.

When Norma Jeane has lived a year and a half with the Goddards, Gladys's condition begins to improve. She shows some interest in the outside world and begins a fragile renewal of goals. Gladys's first goal is to reestablish contact with Berniece and to encourage her to correspond with Norma Jeane. A dramatic new element will be added to Norma Jeane's life, one that will enchant her as a blend of reality and fantasy. Gladys has asked Grace to reveal to Norma Jeane that she has a sister.

Chapter Two

T he few things Berniece knows about her mother have been squeezed, like water from stone, from her father Jasper and her stepmother Maggie.

And Berniece's memories are almost nonexistent. Maggie does her best to answer questions about Gladys, but what Maggie tells seems so little, and Berniece's curiosity grows to frustrating proportions. She has always been fascinated by the small framed photograph on her dresser. Once she had remarked to her father at the great contrast in the appearance of her beautiful mother and the homely Maggie.

"Your mother was a beautiful woman," Jasper had agreed. "But she was also very young, too young to know how to take care of children. That's why I brought you and Jackie to your grandmother—so you'd be taken care of. That's why I married an older lady the next time." He is reluctant to speak further of Gladys.

Berniece had a brother, two years older than she, Robert Kermit, nicknamed Jackie. He had his father's brown hair, his mother's blue eyes, and a never-ending run of bad luck.

Jackie seemed destined for disaster. When he was just tiny, he almost lost an eye. Daddy said that my mother had thrown glass from a broken bottle into the bathroom trash can. He said Jackie reached into the can and was playing with the glass and cut himself up.

Then when Jackie was about three and a half years old and I was almost two, he got hurt again. Daddy told me that Jackie fell out of our car. Daddy and my mother were coming from California to see my grandmother in Flat Lick, Kentucky, riding in an open car. Jackie was sitting in the backseat by himself. My father and mother were arguing about something. With my mother's attention on Daddy, and

9

Daddy's attention on negotiating mountain curves, Jackie fell out of the car and injured his hip.

Jackie's fall onto the highway will cause him to walk with a noticeable limp as he grows up, but it is only one traumatic incident on this ill-fated visit. Gladys goes on a hike with Jasper's younger brother Audrey. They tromp through the woods to the distant top of a mountain and stay all afternoon. Gladys is twenty and voluptuous with a striking combination of blue eyes and hair bleached to flaxen, a color never before seen in Flat Lick, Kentucky. Although Jasper himself is handsome, with warm brown eyes and an elegant Roman nose, he is jealous of his taller, younger brother. When Gladys returns from the mountain hike, Jasper beats her across the back with a bridle until she bleeds. She runs down into town and shows her back to people on the street, crying that she is afraid of her husband.

Maggie Mills, a widow of forty-eight whom Jasper will eventually marry, watches this drama from the window of her grocery store. She is thirteen years Jasper's senior, and their pairing is markedly different from the norm. When Berniece becomes aware of the oddity of it, Maggie replies in nearly the same way as Jasper has done. "Jasper told me his first wife wouldn't cook and she wouldn't clean house. She wouldn't do anything. She just liked to get out and roam around. He decided next time to find somebody older and responsible."

Out of concern for her children, Gladys overcomes her fear of Jasper, and the unhappy parents tolerate each other for the trip back to California. Gladys files for divorce upon arrival. Fourteen months later, in May 1922, Gladys is granted a divorce from Jasper in Los Angeles. She is given custody of her children.

One day Jasper arrives to pick up the children for a weekend outing but instead makes off for Kentucky with them. With this daring abduction accomplished, Jasper begins a sedate life at his mother's house. Because Jackie continues to limp, Jasper takes him to a hospital in Louisville, where doctors encase Jackie's leg in a cast.

While Jackie is living in the Louisville hospital, Gladys appears in Flat Lick, furious and intent on reclaiming her children. Gladys goes to Jasper's sister to ask her aid in stealing Berniece and Jackie, but Myrtle refuses to help. Instead, she races to alert Jasper.

Daddy and my grandmother kept me hidden, and they told my mother that she had better not go to that hospital and bother Jackie. Of course, Mother went anyway. She visited Jackie, but Daddy had told the doctors not to let her take him out. So she stayed in Louisville and got a job as a housekeeper while she waited for Jackie to get better.

While my mother was in Louisville, my father married for the second time, to Maggie Hunter Mills, and we moved from my grandmother's house in Flat Lick. We were living in Harlan when my mother came from Louisville to see how I was being cared for. She told my father and stepmother that she was going back to Los Angeles. Maggie told me that when it was time to say goodbye to me, my mother just stood there and argued with my father instead. So many times my stepmother remarked upon that: "I just don't see how a mother could turn her back and walk away from two children like that."

Jasper regularly travels across the state to Louisville to check on Jackie. After two years, Jackie's cast finally comes off, but one leg is shorter than the other. Treatment must continue; Jackie now alternates between sporadic stays in Harlan and examinations in Louisville. He wears a large patch over part of his leg, a dressing that requires continual changing. The doctor's tentative diagnosis is tuberculosis of the bone.

Jasper moves the family to Middlesboro, and Jackie is brought home to stay. Jackie's bad luck continues. On the Fourth of July, he places a firecracker in the neck of a Coca-Cola bottle and lights it. Berniece and her pals run for cover. Nothing happens. Jackie limps back to relight the firecracker. With a deafening boom, the Coca-Cola bottle explodes into Jackie's face. He loses his right eye.

He should have been left in the hospital. He was doing fine there. He was even having classes for schoolwork there. But my father wanted him home with us and took him out against the doctors' recommendations.

Eventually, so my father said, Jackie's kidneys couldn't carry off the infection from his leg. Daddy should have taken him to the hospital, but he catheterized Jackie himself at home. Finally, Jackie's kidneys failed completely. He died at fourteen and never knew we had not only a mother who was still alive, but a half sister as well.

My curiosity about my mother never went away; it actually grew more intense as time passed—I think maybe because I didn't know for certain that she was alive. At church, on Mother's Day, everyone would wear roses—red if your mother was living, and white if she was dead. I never knew which to wear. On one Mother's Day, when I was about seventeen, I decided she must be dead, so I wore a white rose.

But I was still curious. I felt I had to try to find her . . . without knowing how. My father didn't help me, I felt, because he was married again and didn't want to think about his first wife. He was always reluctant to discuss her. But ever since I had been old enough to want to see her, I had been trying to find her on my own.

By the time I was engaged to Paris, I thought, "I surely would like to know where my mother is before I marry or make some big decision." I had graduated from high school and was visiting my stepmother's niece Mary Mosely in Ohio. Mary was much older than I, more like an aunt, and I felt very comfortable talking to her. I needed someone like that by that time—my father drank excessively and I never could really talk to him. So I talked to Mary about what was on my mind.

I asked her for advice about finding my mother. Since I was a faithful reader of Dr. Crane's advice column in the newspaper, Mary suggested that I write to him. In my letter, I told Dr. Crane that I had been trying for years to find my mother and wondered what I should do. Dr. Crane wrote back and said, "If your mother has not contacted you in all these years, she doesn't want to, or she doesn't need to. You should stop trying to contact her and just proceed to live your life in the manner you choose." So after that, I didn't try to find my mother anymore. Paris and I were in love and had been engaged for two and a half years, so we made plans to go ahead and get married.

On October 7, 1938, at age nineteen, Berniece marries Paris Miracle. Berniece wants to go to college in Berea, Kentucky, where she can work her way through. She readies her plan to get beyond the stifling green walls of mountains. A series of surprises cause her to revise her plans. Nine months and eleven days after her marriage, she will give birth to a baby girl. Even as she is adjusting to the idea of her own approaching motherhood, out of nowhere she regains the mother she feared lost and acquires a sister she never knew she had.

One day in the winter, a few months after I got married, my father sought me out at the Miracles' house where I was visiting. He said, "I don't know if I ought to give you this or not. At first I thought I would never show it to you. Your stepmother and I talked about it. We decided it's your letter." The envelope he handed me was already open.

It was a letter to me from my mother. She had sent it in care of my father's relatives in Flat Lick. It was the only place she knew to send it where it would reach me. My grandmother and my grandfather were dead by then, but the mailman, who knew everybody in that small community, had given it to my father's brother and he had driven to Pineville to deliver it to my father.

In the letter my mother told me that I had a twelve-year old half sister whose name was Norma Jeane. She gave me the address so I could write her if I wanted to. Norma Jeane was living with a friend of my mother's, Grace Goddard, and Doc, Grace's husband.

The letter was written from a mental institution, Agnews State Hospital in San Jose, California. Mother wrote that she had been hospitalized for about six years. Most of the letter was filled with begging me to help her get out. She also gave me the address of Della's sister, Dora Hogan Graham, who lived in Portland, Oregon. Mother hoped that her Aunt Dora could help her get out.

13

Berniece is overcome with the news in the wrinkled letter. She sighs nervously and hands the letter around to members of the Miracle family. She wants to appear composed, but her chin begins to tremble, and when the tears come, they stream.

Berniece attempts to make sense of this news. It conjures up ancient memories. They are defiantly sparse, unraveled threads, torn spiderwebs. How to connect?

She remembers a windy bridge and a fairhaired stranger.

Her mind focuses upon patches of bright colors—toys arriving in a box from the mailman. This memory is fifteen years old when Gladys's letter arrives.

Berniece can't sleep. She lies in bed with her hands resting against her lightly swelling belly. It takes Berniece several days to assimilate the new fact that she has a mother and a sister. She is proud. She is excited. Tentative feelings of sadness are crowded out by the joy of having mysteries solved. Now she energetically outlines a schedule of letters to compose. As she sets her pen to the first letter, she begins a pattern of long-distance involvement that will cover most of the next twenty-five years.

Berniece writes first to Grace, explaining during the course of the letter that Jackie died. Grace is the first to answer. Her lengthy letter overflows with facts about Norma Jeane and the details of their lives in California. Grace revels in letter writing. Norma Jeane uses the name Baker, Grace explains, because her father died before she was born. Gladys reverted to Baker so that all her children would have the same last name—part of her dream is to have all her children together with her. Grace closes by touching upon the possibility of Norma Jeane's going to Kentucky to visit Berniece and Paris.

14

Grace told me she had decided years before that it wasn't her place to try to contact me. She continually hoped that Gladys would accept that as her own responsibility and so was delighted when Mother finally decided to get in touch. In my letter to Norma Jeane, I sent a snapshot, and right away she wrote back and sent me one of herself.

Norma Jeane's letters to Berniece are sweet and neatly written. She fills pages with the chummy tidbits of a twelve-year old: favorite movies, favorite songs, descriptions and sketches of hairstyles she and Grace's stepdaughter Bebe might try out, requests for more snapshots, questions about Kentucky ("My

teacher said Daniel Boone passed through your town—did he?")
Norma Jeane's handwriting is careful and controlled, vertical
with no forward slant to it. She signs the letters, "Your sister."

*Next I wrote Mother's Aunt Dora in Oregon and asked her if she
would help get my mother out of the institution. She wanted much
more information and needed time to consider it all. Aunt Dora
eventually got Mother released from Agnews State Hospital in San
Jose.*

*Then I wrote to my mother and told her I had written the others
and that I would try to get her out of the institution. I told her I was
ecstatic to learn that I had a little sister.*

Gladys's reply to Berniece is a scathing criticism of mental
institutions. Gladys, now about thirty-eight years old, fills
ten pages with her feelings about the horrors of confinement.
She gives Berniece detailed instructions on how to put a bill
through Congress to get the institutions changed. Like leaflets
dropped from an airplane, Gladys's letters begin to shower upon
Berniece.

At first, Berniece shows them all to Paris's father, Wilbourn,
a former teacher who has named his children after characters in
classical mythology. He is presently a railroad telegraph agent
and a master of the mysterious Morse Code, so Wilbourn is
regarded as the sage of the family. "The anger and frustration
in these letters are painful to see," he comments. "The train of
thought seems to be a hodgepodge mingling of religious dogma
with paranoid delusions. It's terribly confusing and illogical.
Maybe she had brain damage."

The letters pile up in a box, which moves with Paris and
Berniece to their second rented house and then to a new guest
cottage built by Wilbourn. Most will be lost in the great floods of
the Cumberland River.

15

A ponderous Berniece trudges into the Miracles' yard at twilight, smiling a tired hello to her mother-in-law, Rachel. Berniece is grimy, itching, and weary from a boat ride to Paris's vegetable garden across the river. Her formerly slim figure is now distorted to 150 pounds in the ninth month of her pregnancy. Rachel tells Berniece that Grace and Doc Goddard have passed through Pineville on their way to West Virginia, hoping to meet Berniece and to arrange for her to meet her sister, perhaps to arrange a move for Norma Jeane. It is July 1939. Berniece will celebrate her twentieth birthday on July 30. As Berniece leaves her teens, Norma Jeane is entering hers, having turned thirteen years old on June 1.

Grace must have been dismayed at our situation. She could see the town, our two room apartment down the street. Whatever plan she might have been entertaining about Norma Jeane's coming to live with me, I'm sure she abandoned.

After Doc's West Virginia assignment, he and Grace return to California and Grace becomes back fence friends with Ethel Dougherty. Doc's daughter Bebe and Norma Jeane have noticed that a handsome young man lives in the Dougherty house on Archwood Street. But Jim Dougherty—eighteen, a senior in Van Nuys High School, president of the student body, and a member of the Maskers dramatic club—is out of the girls' orbit. When Jim graduates from high school and settles into a job at Lockheed Aircraft, the five year age difference between him and Norma Jeane might as well be five light-years. His notice of her has been mainly confined to shouting out of his bedroom window to stifle her shrieking as she rolls on the ground, playing with the Goddards' dog.

Fate, however, and the guiding hand of Grace, arrange that Norma Jeane and Jim begin a friendship. The Goddards move too far from school for the girls to continue to walk, and Grace asks Jim to help. Jim is free in the daytime, since he works the graveyard shift at Lockheed, and agrees to give Bebe and Norma Jeane daily rides.

Norma Jeane spends Sundays at the house of Grace's Aunt Ana. Norma Jeane idolizes Aunt Ana, goes to the Christian Science church with her, and becomes an adherent of the faith in which Ana is a professional lay counselor, or practitioner. After Ana moves to her rental property on Nebraska Avenue in West Los Angeles, the Goddard family moves into her house on Odessa Street in Van Nuys, agreeing to make mortgage payments to her.

When Doc's company holds its Christmas dance in December 1941, Grace asks Jim to be Norma Jeane's escort and to find a buddy of his for Bebe. Norma Jeane is fifteen. She begins dating Jim, and by spring she tells Grace and Ana that she is in love with him. When Doc is transferred to West Virginia, Norma Jeane chooses to remain in California. She moves in with her adored Aunt Ana in February 1942, enrolling for second semester at University High School. Ethel Dougherty and Grace confer about the romance between Jim and Norma Jeane. They decide to encourage the couple to get married. Jim likes the idea. He will later say that Norma Jeane was the most mature sixteen year-old he ever knew. Ana handles all the arrangements for the June wedding, including the invitations.

Berniece senses something unique about the envelope she lifts from her mailbox. It is the first she has seen from the hand of Ana Lower. Norma Jeane is getting married, announces Ana. Pillowcases will make a nice and useful gift, she suggests. Ana encloses a formal invitation for the wedding of Norma Jeane Baker and James Dougherty, scheduled to take place on June 9, 1942.

Crunching cinders sound the rhythm of Berniece's haste along the roadway as her daughter Mona Rae runs ahead. Once inside, Berniece sniffs, then laughs at herself as she brushes away two quick tears.

"What's the matter, toots?" demands Niobe as she takes hold of her friend.

"Well, good news, really. My sister is getting married. I got the invitation today."

"Ah . . . your daddy . . ." mutters Niobe.

"I haven't been down there yet. He wouldn't really be interested."

"Want me to walk down there with you?"

"After Paris gets home, I'll go. Maybe . . . after supper. I don't know . . . I don't know what I feel."

Norma Jeane's wedding takes place in the home of Chester Howell, an attorney friend of the Goddards, three weeks after Norma Jeane's sixteenth birthday. Norma Jeane, beautiful and elegant in a long white gown, is a classic bride. A high school classmate is her maid of honor; Jim's older brother Marion is the best man; his sister Billie's little son Wes is ring bearer. Rev. Charles Lingenfelder, a family friend of the Doughertys, performs the rites.

The reception was held at the Howell home—not, as has been said, at the Florentine Gardens where Norma Jeane supposedly danced in a conga line and a waiter spilled ketchup on Jim's white tuxedo.

Jim praised Norma Jeane as lover, homemaker, and friend in his memoir, The Secret Happiness of Marilyn Monroe, *and he related that Norma Jeane was a virgin when they married, though the myth continues that she was raped in one of a series of foster homes.*

Jim says Norma Jeane is an immaculate housekeeper and a versatile cook whose dishes include wild game. In whatever she takes on, she strives for perfection. She tucks love notes in Jim's lunch box, and later, when he is at sea for a year, she posts more than two hundred letters to him. A friend gives the couple a collie, Mugsie, and Norma Jeane bathes the pet nearly every day. Their movie going is infrequent; Norma Jeane and Jim spend much of their free time outdoors—shooting, fishing, swimming, boating. At gatherings with friends Jim plays the guitar and Norma Jeane sings. Every Sunday they attend the Sherman Oaks

Christian Science Church. Norma Jeane delights in taking care of Jim's nieces and nephews, and the children adore her.

The only threat to the newlyweds' happiness seems to be an external one. Hanging over them is the possibility that Jim may be drafted.

In 1942, with Mona Rae almost three years old, Berniece and Paris consider moving to some northern industrial city to improve their financial prospects. World War II is a major force shaping lives now, creating opportunities along with disruptions.

Paris works three days a week at Baird's Grocery. He is also a volunteer fireman. He would also be working in a coal mine, but at that Berniece has drawn the line. Berniece burns to get past these mountains.

"Everybody with any sense has left this place—if the army hasn't already caught them," Berniece declares. "You can't make a living here."

Berniece has been able to channel some of her pentup energy and frustration into sewing. She makes clothes for herself and Mona Rae. Paris brings home empty feed sacks from work. Berniece turns the floral print muslin into shorts and blouses. Like all the neighbors, they have a vegetable garden in the backyard. Now it is called a Victory Garden. Already Berniece has decided to limit their financial burdens by rearing one child only.

Berniece leaves Mona Rae with Rachel, happily layering sliced bananas and Vanilla Wafers into a pudding, and Berniece and Niobe escape for their cheapest entertainment—walking. They cross the rickety bridge and walk the road following the river's abrupt twist to the north where a sign reads Highway 25E. This is the highway along which so many young couples have fled, determined to make new starts, some stopping in Louisvillle, some venturing on to Cincinnati, and some following rumors of opportunities all the way to Detroit.

But Paris's father Wilbourn is building a guest cottage at the back edge of his property for Paris and Berniece. He creates the concrete blocks himself, each one with twin mounds on its outside surface, and with a flourish he sets a varicolored marble

19

into the peak of each mound. They look like breasts with blue, green, gold, and red nipples.

Paris's dad was building with such care, I wondered how we could tell him we had to leave, that we could not live in the little house. I was dreaming again, of course. We would move into it and be grateful.

Until we could find a way out.

erniece and Paris have moved their family to Detroit when a letter arrives postmarked February 2, 1944 from Catalina Island, where Norma Jeane is living with her "Jimmie." He is stationed there with the maritime service, training for the merchant marine.

Norma Jeane thanks Berniece for the picture she sent of her and Paris, saying, "I just can't tell you how much you look like Mother. I was so surprised, I could hardly speak." She writes that their mother's eyes aren't as dark as Berniece's, but their other features are very much the same. Norma Jeane says she has their mother's eyes, forehead and hairline, but otherwise she looks like her dad.

"Also," she adds, "I had no idea that Paris was so nice looking." She says she keeps the picture on her bookshelf and when people ask about the nice looking couple, "I explain proudly that that is my sister and her husband."

Norma Jeane goes on to tell Berniece about Catalina Island, remembering a time when she was seven years old and their mother brought her to a dance at the Casino there. She says that recently the maritime service held a dance at the same place.

She gets seasick on the boat ride from Los Angeles, but seems to like the island. She wishes that Berniece, Paris, and Mona Rae could come visit: "I know that once you get here you wouldn't want to leave, at least that's what most people say. And I do want to see you all very much and I know Mother would too."

Norma Jeane adds a gentle persuasion that if Paris fears he might be drafted, he should enroll in the maritime service and then perhaps they can all be together.

The idyll on Catalina ends when Jim is shipped out for sea duty. Norma Jeane moves in with Jim's parents, who now live on Hermitage Street. Before the Goddards left West Virginia,

21

Doc Goddard helped Ethel Dougherty get a job at Radio Plane, a defense plant, where she works in the infirmary. Norma Jeane asks Ethel if there is a chance she, too, might be hired on. Norma Jeane begins work as an assembly line chute packer, then as a glue sprayer. As in all her endeavors, she strives for perfection. She wins a certificate for excellence, but the ego boost is counteracted by her coworkers' envy.

More intense than the reaction to her certificate for excellence is the resentment when an army photographer comes into the plant to do a layout featuring women in war work for *Yank* magazine. Photographer David Conover's discovery of an evanescent natural model transforms this routine assignment in a drab location into an inspired one. Posing for three days creates a focus for Norma Jeane's inchoate yearnings. David Conover shows the photos to a photographer friend, Potter Hueth, who is even more excited than Conover. Hueth shoots a series of Norma Jeane and shows them to Emmeline Snively, owner of the Blue Book Modeling Agency. After poring over a brochure Emmeline sends her, Norma Jeane enrolls in her three-month modeling course under an agreement to pay the fee with earnings from jobs Emmeline will arrange for her.

When Jim first went to sea, Norma Jeane had time on her hands. Now she has an overload of activities: job, evening classes, modeling assignments. At times, she must call in sick at Radio Plane to go on assignments. Norma Jeane moves from the Doughertys' home back into the home of Aunt Ana, who is rather more accepting of her new interest than are her in-laws. Eventually Norma Jeane earns enough to quit Radio Plane. Her budding career during the next two years includes jobs as photographer's model, hostess at industrial shows and celebrity events, and model for calendar artist Earl Moran.

None of this happens suddenly, however. Norma Jeane does not make an impetuous commitment, nor is she bombarded with jobs. Her ambition is still embryonic. She is sorting things out, deciding who she is, weighing what she wants. She decides to take a break from everything. It is an opportune time to go and meet Berniece.

Even the hope of getting together with Norma Jeane was a dream to me, but when Grace came to Detroit, where we had moved, I saw that a visit was within the realm of possibility.

Paris and I went to join Grace and Doc one night for dinner at the Cadillac Hotel. It was the first time Grace had ever seen me, and she hugged me and hugged me until I was breathless. It seemed like she was pouring out affection that she had been saving for years.

Berniece finds this quick little woman with the soprano voice immensely likable and as newsy in person as she has been in her letters. While Paris and Doc analyze Ford Motors and Detroit's other defense plants, Berniece and Grace explore family relationships.

Berniece tells Grace that Mona Rae is rather small for her age. Grace smiles at the photo Berniece hands her. "Petite. Like her grandmother Gladys."

"My mother is little?" asks Berniece.

"About my size. About five feet" nods Grace. "When we roomed together, we could wear some of each other's clothes."

Grace explains that Gladys had to work after Norma Jeane was born, so she stayed with a family across the street from Berniece's grandmother's house for a while. Later, when Gladys bought her own place, she took Norma Jeane to live with her and put her in school nearby.

"Gladys was making good money. And she brought in an English family to share the house and help with the housekeeping. They stayed until we found out they were treating Norma Jeane unkindly and we got rid of them. The happy days didn't last long."

In a few months, it was in 1934, Gladys had her nervous breakdown."

Berniece looks up at Grace. "Did my mother suddenly . . . did she just . . . how did it happen?"

"Well, as I said, Gladys was making good money. We were both at Columbia then, but we knew there were going to be strikes and depressions right around the corner. I told her not to buy it. I begged her not to buy it." Grace pauses and begins on her wilting salad. "Gladys said she wanted to have a place so she

23

could have all her children together. Norma Jeane and you and Jackie."

"So she bought it anyway?"

"Yes. And then, sure enough, there was a strike," Grace continues. "Gladys and another girl climbed over the fence and went to work anyway. Their picture got in the newspaper."

"So she kept working."

"Oh, yes," Grace nods her head, remembering. "It seemed like a lot of things happened all at once to put pressure on her. Overwork . . . the trouble with the English couple. And then the studio laid off a lot of employees . . . Gladys was laid off."

"Then, when it started," Grace tries to explain, "I don't know . . . it built up very fast, her illness. The first I saw of it, one day she was lying on the couch and she—there were steps in the living room leading upstairs—she started kicking and yelling, staring up at the staircase. She would lie there on her back and yell, 'Somebody's coming down those steps to kill me!' She was having delusions." Grace pauses a moment. "The house and all the responsibilities were just too much for her."

"She lost the house?"

"Oh yes! The house and the furniture were auctioned. My Aunt Ana saved the piano. She bought it and finished making payments on it."

"And that's when you were made my mother's guardian?"

"When she went into the institution, I became her guardian. And Norma Jeane's. She was in a private hospital until the money ran out, and then she was sent up to Agnews, the state institution. Yes, everything just fell through for her."

"And then Norma Jeane lived with you and Aunt Ana?"

"Not then, honey, no. I tried to keep her, but my schedule . . . I couldn't keep her. I had to put her in the orphanage."

"The orphanage!"

"She was there over a year. And then after Doc and I got married, I got her out and she stayed with us. Norma Jeane was with us until Doc transferred to Huntington, and then she wanted to stay with my Aunt Ana and get ready to marry Jimmy."

"Norma Jeane seems real happy, from her letters," Paris comments to Doc.

"Yes, she does," agrees Doc. "She and Jimmy are two kids in love."

"She seems to be crazy about Catalina Island," Paris says. "She's trying to recruit me to the merchant marine."

"That was a lucky assignment for Jimmy," Doc nods.

"Norma Jeane sounds so sweet in her letters," exclaims Berniece. "I'd just give anything to be able to see her."

"It would be wonderful," agrees Grace.

"And my mother . . . I keep hoping . . ."

"We're all praying, dear," Grace nods.

Chapter Five

*J*ust a few months later, in the backseat of a blue Pontiac, Norma Jeane and Berniece lean across Mona Rae, squashing her. They stare into each other's faces and then laugh at their impulse to stare. They spoke to each other in person, saw each other in the flesh for the first time less than an hour before. Overcome with excitement, they hug once again. Five year old Mona Rae extricates herself from between the two women and scrambles onto the ledge behind the backseat.

To Berniece, it hardly seems right to whisk Norma Jeane from the train station directly to their cramped apartment in the Polish district. She wonders if some kind of protocol is in order but hardly knows what to do on this great occasion. Paris follows a half discussed plan for a sightseeing ride. He steers the old Pontiac through Detroit streets, past public buildings, department stores, skyscrapers, and parks. Then he drives across the river into Canada, acting as guide on a formless tour to see sights that no one seems to be looking at. Beside Paris sits his sister Niobe. Both of them twist around constantly to peer into the backseat.

It is the autumn of 1944, and Norma Jeane is eighteen. While Jim is on sea duty with the merchant marine, she has blown her wife's allotment money on the trip to Detroit.

Every time Norma Jeane and I wrote letters, we talked about wanting to get together, but it was really Grace who coordinated this visit. After Grace and Doc made their trip to Detroit, Grace felt it was high time for Norma Jeane and me to get together.

When Grace wrote me that a visit was possible, I answered her—she was living in West Virginia then—and said, "Sure! I'd love to have Norma Jeane, love to! My husband's sister Niobe is up here now, but we'll make room anyway." Grace said Norma Jeane could stay indefinitely so we went right out and bought a little army cot for her. And then Norma Jeane wrote and told me that she'd be there, what train, what time, everything.

Norma Jeane had written to tell me what kind of outfit she would be wearing and what color it would be. Paris and Niobe and I walked out to the tracks and stood waiting while the train screeched to a stop. I wondered which one of us would recognize her first, or if we might possibly miss her. Well, there was no chance of missing her! All the passengers stepping off looked so ordinary, and then, all of a sudden, there was this tall, gorgeous girl. All of us shouted at once. None of the other passengers looked anything like that: tall, so pretty and fresh, and wearing what she had described, a cobalt blue wool suit and a hat with a heart shaped dip in the brim.

Berniece instinctively scans for physical resemblances. She notes Norma Jeane's eyes at once; in contrast with her own brown ones, Norma Jeane's almost match the cobalt blue of her suit. Perhaps the blue of Gladys's eyes is the same, Berniece thinks. Berniece sees her own mouth repeated on Norma Jeane's face, the same front teeth, large, unusually white, and just an attractive millimeter away from protruding. Berniece is struck that their hair is nearly the same dark blond and that the strands wave off their foreheads from a widow's peak in the same pattern.

They embrace each other. And weep. And laugh. The photographs Norma Jeane sent to Paris and Berniece have not captured her essence. Her beauty is natural, vibrantly fresh. An abundant cascade of waves frames a porcelain fair face. Her cheeks glow with a faint blush. Her smile is untrained, spontaneous, friendly. Her body is slender, neither plump nor voluptuous, emanating simply a delicious ripeness.

It is Norma Jeane's inner presence, however, that captivates the four who have come to greet her. Her little niece Mona Rae, with a child's infallible radar, immediately trusts the new aunt. A thought too mysterious and complicated for the adults to articulate is expressed without hesitation by the child: "She's pretty and sweet and soft, and she smells good and I feel good when she hugs me."

27

We drove around showing her some of Detroit, and then somehow the car was headed toward Canada. I really dreaded taking her to our dinky apartment.

Some of the time all four of us were talking at once, and some of the time nobody was saying a word. Instead of sitting back to relax in the car, Norma Jeane and I sort of perched in the edge of the seat at an angle so we could stare at each other. Every now and then our arms would fly around each other in a hug and we'd look in each other's eyes and say how happy we were. We didn't have anything very original or profound to say. We were both so excited we were almost out of our minds; we were hardly aware of what was going on. The two of us were just . . . we sat there like two people who had just fallen in love, I guess. We were overwhelmed at finally getting to see each other. I was so proud of her.

They go to Miner's Bird Sanctuary in Kingsville, Ontario. A jungle of green leaves surrounds them. Broad splashes of color—orange, white, blue, chartreuse—move erratically and cry out. Tiny strokes of yellow twitter and chirp. Norma Jeane's refrain punctuates the bird music: "I'm so happy! Take a picture of us with these birds, Niobe. Can we take pictures here? Can you believe it—this is my first time out of the United States! Let's take a picture of us while we're in Canada!" The youthful excitement of the group ebbs only slightly when the aimless tour ends, inevitably, at home.

Berniece and Paris have made their way beyond the walls of mountains and are now surrounded by walls of concrete. Paris works at Ford and Berniece at De Soto. Mona Rae spends the days at nursery school. Niobe has become part of the Detroit household, sleeping on the living room couch, grateful to be in training at Chrysler.

Tonight they cross the plank walkway to the back of the house without complaint, and laughter fills the stairwell leading to their three room apartment.

"Well, as you can see," groans Berniece with a resigned grin and a sweep of her arm, "the kitchen and the living room are one and the same."

28

"Oh, I'm used to small quarters." Norma Jeane giggles. "I used to sleep in a drawer."

"In a what?" asks Paris.

"In a drawer! Grace told me that when mother brought me home from the hospital—Grace and Mother hadn't been living together for a while, and Grace didn't even know I had been born; in fact, nobody did—well, anyway, Mother didn't have a crib to put me in, so she pulled out the dresser drawer in her bedroom and made me a little bed in the drawer."

Berniece notices Norma Jeane's occasional stammer and decides she must put aside this foolish self consciousness about their apartment and concentrate on putting Norma Jeane at ease.

They begin to compare resemblances again. Berniece wants to look at feet. They call Mona Rae over. The three of them line up their feet side by side and remark upon the length of their toes. The middle toe is the longest, like the middle finger on a hand. So amusing is this common feature that they laugh like delighted maniacs, exhausted and slaphappy.

They relax and begin to leisurely weave together the threads of their lives. Berniece has had to leave cartons of letters and memorabilia stored in Pineville, but from a small box in a dresser drawer she fishes out a photograph and hands it gingerly to Norma Jeane.

29

"Daddy gave me this picture of my mother. I kept it on my dresser all through school. Have you ever seen this?" The photograph shows a beautiful young woman of undetermined age. Between fifteen and twenty, Gladys has the same dark blond waves flowing from her forehead as do her daughters, and soft ringlets fall to the back of a slender neck.

"What does she look like now?" Berniece asks. "Is she still pretty?"

"Mother's still fairly pretty" replies Norma Jeane. "But she never smiles. I drove up with Aunt Ana to see her at the institution. I almost wish I hadn't. I hadn't seen her in ten years and I was expecting . . . I was looking forward . . . she wasn't . . . I didn't go again. She's not like my mother. Grace is like my mother. And Aunt Ana, even more than Grace."

"What do you remember about Mother when you were little?"

"I don't remember too much really," says Norma Jeane and sighs. "She's really a blur to me. I remember her taking me to school, though. She dressed me in a cute sailor outfit . . . a little white pleated skirt with a navy middy blouse. I remember going to school . . . I remember a little bit about the house we had . . . when I went to live with her, when I was seven—oh, and the piano!" Norma Jeane exclaims. A happy note replaces the tiredness in her voice. "I sat at a huge black piano, and I took lessons. It's at Aunt Ana's now. There was an auction, and she saved it for me. It's a very special piano—it used to belong to Fredric March—but I really can't play. Nothing much. Do you play the piano?"

"Oh, I used to try," chuckles Berniece. "I played a little. But I did play the French horn in high school."

"You liked music a lot, didn't you, Berniece? Did you sing, too?"

"Mmm . . . no, not really. Well, just in church. And then once in a talent show."

"Really? You did? I did, too. I did a tap dance and sang to 'College Rhythm.'"

"'College Rhythm'?" cries Berniece. "You didn't! 'College Rhythm'! That's what I did. Exactly!"

"Oh, Berniece, you and I did exactly the same thing?" whispers Norma Jeane. She stares at Berniece like a round eyed statue.

"Goodnight girls! Goodnight!" Paris's voice from the bedroom reminds them that tomorrow is a workday. "You'll have the neighbors banging their brooms on the ceiling."

"Well, anyway," Norma Jeane whispers, "you asked me about Mother. As I was starting to say, she's really a stranger to me. Almost as much a stranger as she is to you. Part of me wants to be with her . . . and part of me is a little afraid of her."

Berniece nods and pats Norma Jeane's hand. "That's understandable, sure."

Norma Jeane continues, "I went to see Mother because she seemed to have regained some interest in the outside world. You know, she'd told us about each other and she's been wanting to get out of the institution. But the plain fact is she has never actually said to me, 'Come visit me,' just things like, 'Get me out.'"

"We will get her out, Norma Jeane. We'll just keep working at it, and praying about it." Berniece makes herself smile, wanting to feel optimistic. "Grace and Aunt Dora Graham say she acts a lot better these days." Berniece pats Norma Jeane's hand again. "You're exhausted. We'd better get some sleep."

"Mmm hmm," Norma Jeane makes a sleepy clown's face. "I guess I'd better. But you and Paris and Niobe are the ones who have to go to work tomorrow."

"Berniece, you're not letting me do anything! Let me do some cooking for us," demands Norma Jeane. "I'll make us dinner—it's a simple dish. You probably have the stuff in the cupboard."

Norma Jeane's specialty turns out to be peas and carrots. She likes to mix them because of the bright contrast of orange and green. Berniece will eventually see this small cooking idiosyncrasy repeated endlessly in movie magazines. Dismayed in future years at the fabrications in magazine stories, Berniece will comment, "That part, at least, is true."

Norma Jeane talked continually about the merchant marine, trying to get Paris to commit himself to going to California and joining up.

Before Jim had gone into the merchant marine, he had been a supervisor at Lockheed Aircraft, and even then Norma Jeane was writing to us suggesting that Jim might be able to help Paris get a job there if only we would come out to California.

When we made the choice of Detroit, it was because people we knew had gotten jobs there in defense plants when the war started and because Detroit was fairly close to Pineville—home. Nevertheless, Norma Jeane wasn't about to consider as closed the possibility of our moving to California.

Chapter Six

"At least you have a father," Norma Jeane says with a sigh. Berniece is giving her a manicure and pushes gently at Norma Jeane's cuticle with an orange stick. "What's your father like, Berniece?" Berniece has taken the day off from De Soto, and these rare hours alone together have allowed them to discuss family matters in leisure and privacy.

"Daddy's . . . well, we're not too close, really." Berniece sighs as wistfully as Norma Jeane. "He has always had a drinking problem, it seems. He was good to me, I guess. He tried awfully hard to make a living. Let me get his picture for you."

Norma Jeane studies the photograph that Berniece fishes out of her small box. "He's rather handsome," Norma Jeane judges. "He looks sort of like Burgess Meredith. He must have seemed very romantic to Mother. She was just seventeen when they married and him a handsome older man."

"He was in the cavalry," Berniece says. "He used to ride five or six horses at one time. He would jump from one horse to the other."

"Sounds like he was in the circus!" Norma Jeane giggles.

"He stayed on in California when he was discharged. He got some apartments—that's how he met our mother. Her mother managed the apartments for him. And also he ran a concession down on the beach—throwing balls, bingo, dice, games like they have in carnivals, you know. He said our mother helped him with it when they were first married."

"Had he been a farmer back in Kentucky?" asks Norma Jeane.

Berniece laughs. "No, he was never a farmer. Everything but. Let me have your other hand now." Berniece blows a stream of air across the wet scarlet fingernails on Norma Jeane's left hand. "He went into the service right after he finished school. He just took off and enlisted," Berniece continues.

"Years later, after he came back to Kentucky with Jackie and me, he took state examinations and got a teaching certificate. In those days, if you had passed certain grades, you could teach those grades."

"From circus performer to teacher," says Norma Jeane. "Wow! What a change! Did he like teaching?"

"I guess not. He never stuck with the jobs long."

Berniece leans back, squinting at Norma Jeane's right hand draped across her own, examining the nails for uniform length.

"Then, after the teaching," Berniece continues, "Daddy and Ma Baker ran Happy Jack's Pool Room."

"Happy Jack's! What a cute name," says Norma Jeane. "Hey, was the pool room named after Jackie?"

"No, and his real name wasn't John or Jack at all. It was Robert Kermit."

"Was it like your dad was big Jack and Robert was little Jackie?"

"You know, I'm not sure where 'Happy Jack' came from because Daddy's nickname wasn't Jack. People called him Jap—shortened from Jasper."

"Our brother," begins Norma Jeane. "You know, I don't think Mother thinks Jackie is really dead. Grace told me when she visited Mother after you had written her and told her he was dead, that she refused to believe it."

"Well," Berniece hesitates, "I guess . . . I'm sure . . . well, naturally Mother wouldn't want her son to be dead, and in her condition . . . being confused about reality."

"Why do you think when Mother first wrote from Agnews that she wrote to you instead of to Jackie—after all, he was older than you—or why she didn't write to the two of you together?"

"I don't know. Perhaps, in her confusion, Mother thought Jackie was still in the hospital in Louisville. For that matter, she didn't even really know where I might be. She sent the letter to Daddy's people in Flat Lick. Don't you agree, she wouldn't necessarily be logical?"

Norma Jeane nods. "Because of her condition."

Norma Jeane and Berniece hear footsteps on the plank walkway.

"Well," says Berniece looking at her watch, "that must be Paris and Niobe."

"Hello, hello, you two ladies of leisure!" calls Niobe from the stairwell.

Paris strolls in with Mona Rae astride his hip. Drooping upside down like a monkey, Mona Rae swings out to plant kisses on the cheeks of Norma Jeane and Berniece.

"Remember, we're going out to eat tonight, honey," Berniece reminds Paris.

"I know" he answers, and surveys the array of tiny bottles of polish, wooden sticks, and metal implements. He clutches his stomach, indicating hunger. "How long?"

"About twenty minutes." Berniece smiles. "And don't jiggle me again, please." Paris obliges by shadow boxing at her ribs, and Berniece aims her tiny brush with its dollop of scarlet at him in a mock threat. "You and Niobe go fight over the bathroom. Norma Jeane and I have already been in there."

"Hold still now," Berniece warns Norma Jeane, whose hand has started to shake as she laughs at their sparring. "So anyway, Daddy's next venture was to rent houses in Wallsend. Then the floods started getting in our house, ruining everything we had. Bless his heart, Daddy tried to haul stuff up to the attic, then the floodwater rose clear up to the roof, and everything was ruined anyway. I lost all my letters from you and Mother."

"That's why we call it 'World's End', instead of Wallsend," Paris adds.

"How awful," says Norma Jeane. "How can people stay in a town if there's a danger of floods?"

"They're more or less trapped," Berniece answers. "Who would buy their property, knowing it would be flooded?"

"Nobody stays there if they can help it," Niobe declares.

Once they're dressed for their evening out, they troop down the back stairway and across the plank walkway. Norma Jeane wears her blue traveling suit with a fresh white blouse. As they climb into the car and adjust themselves, the conversation comes back to the subject of Jasper.

"Well, your daddy sounds like a pretty good person," muses Norma Jeane. "He's had a pretty tough life."

"I guess so. He drank too much, most of the time. But there were a few good times. He always let me have a car to take the girls riding. But I never could talk to him about things.

"I remember," Berniece continues, "when I was getting to be about thirteen or fourteen, he would say, 'Now don't you let any of the boys feel all over you.' He told me when I married somebody to be sure and marry somebody who had a little money. Not to marry somebody who didn't have anything."

"She started going with me about that time," chuckles Paris. "And Jasper told her, 'Paris Miracle doesn't have anything, nor his daddy, none of their people have anything.' But we got married anyway," Paris continues with a grin, "because my daddy had told me to marry for money, too! So I married Berniece for her money!"

"Paris Miracle!" Berniece shrieks.

Niobe laughs until she begins to choke.

"Did you, Daddy?" asks Mona Rae. From her perch on the rear window ledge, she makes a slithering dive across Berniece and Norma Jeane. Then she begins to pound upon Aunt Niobe's shoulders to relieve her coughing.

Norma Jeane leans against the door, one hand upon her midsection, eyes closed and crinkled with amusement. "You're quite a storyteller, Paris!"

On the way to dinner, they circle through the suburb of Dearborn, and in the course of the evening they show Norma Jeane all three work locations—Chrysler, Ford, and De Soto—which are now operating as defense plants. Norma Jeane has worked in a factory herself, and she groans, "Ugh, these buildings look about the same as Radio Plane in California."

Chapter Seven

"*I*'ve never understood quite what Mother's talking about in her letters," says Berniece. "I mean . . . I'm sure it's okay. You know, I guess Aunt Ana told you, that she wrote and asked me if I would like for her to visit Mother in the institution and encourage her in Christian Science."

Norma Jeane nods, "Aunt Ana said you thought it would be good because some kind of faith should be helpful to her."

"Yes. But Aunt Ana also told me that Christian Science ideas might cause a problem later on. I know it's a different kind of religion, yet I don't see how it could possibly cause a problem."

"I studied it, too," says Norma Jeane.

"You did! Oh, tell me some things."

"Well, it is different. For instance, Scientists don't say grace before meals like people in other faiths do. Also, Christmas is not important—it's celebrated, but it's not a major occasion. Scientists are supposed to study a lot. There are rooms where you can go to read. They're like little libraries. Grace and Doc, by the way, are not Scientists."

Norma Jeane grows self confident and voluble, talking about a subject with which she is familiar and comfortable. Her stammer disappears for a time, but it is a characteristic that persists for the duration of Norma Jeane's stay. Berniece has concluded that it signifies Norma Jeane's insecurity and desire to be accepted.

"The main book," explains Norma Jeane, "is *Science and Health with Key to the Scriptures*, by Mary Baker Eddy. She started Christian Science. In that book, you can learn how to change your thinking. And there are practitioners to help you with your problems. Aunt Ana is one. Scientists believe in mind over matter. Mind causes disease. Mind also cures disease. They don't believe in taking medicines."

"Never?"

"Never. That's one way problems could arise. A doctor could say that somebody should have a blood transfusion and the patient might be a Scientist and not want a transfusion and a non-scientist in the family might insist that the patient should have it. Things like that."

"Then if you're in Christian Science, you don't take any medicines? Not aspirins or anything?"

"No." Norma Jeane shakes her head, then realizes that Berniece is referring to her personally. "Oh, you mean me? Well, I'm not too good at practicing that part of it. I take . . . prescriptions, stuff for cramps. I did better when I lived with Aunt Ana before I married Jimmy. But she still helps me. I probably have too many other things on my mind now. But Aunt Ana really is an inspiration. Did you like your stepmother?"

"Oh, yes. Very much. She's been very good to me. She taught me things and brought me up. She didn't have any children of her own, and she was thrilled to be called Mama. I remember that once Jackie told somebody that she wasn't his real mother and it upset her terribly."

"That reminds me of Aunt Ida Bolender," smiles Norma Jeane. "Aunt Ida told me she had to teach me not to call her Mama because Mother had gotten upset hearing me do that. And I got totally confused after that and thought "mama" just meant "woman." I missed Aunt Ida when I went to live with Mother. I was just seven."

37

"You liked her? She was a good person?"

"Oh, yes. I was very lucky to have her. She and Uncle Wayne came to my wedding."

"I always felt that way about my stepmother, too," Berniece says. "As time goes on, I look back and appreciate her even more."

"How about Mother's parents, Norma Jeane, our Monroe grandparents—Did you know them?"

"Oh, good gracious, no." Norma Jeane sighs. "They were dead way before my time. I think my grandfather was from McCreed, Missouri . . . they were from Missouri. My grandfather died when Mother was eight or nine years old, I think, and my grandmother died when I was about a year old."

"I wonder why Mother didn't let our grandmother keep you instead of putting you with the Bolenders."

Norma Jeane considers the idea. Above her nose appears a slight crease of puzzlement. She replies, "I guess my grandmother just was too sick with malaria to keep me. When she went to Borneo with her husband—not my grandfather, he was dead—she got malaria. They told me she was often delirious with fevers. She died from malaria."

"Borneo! I have a postcard she sent me from there, a postcard with a picture of a huge snake on it. Her husband then was . . ."

"Grainger. Say, did you know that my real grandfather was related to President Monroe?"

"Gee, really?" exclaims Berniece. "No, I didn't. Hey, that means I am, too! He's my grandfather, too!"

"Right! That's what Grace said Mother told her."

"I guess that ought to hold me for a while, finding out I'm related to a president!" Bernice exclaims.

"But it won't," she warns, regaining composure. "I'm a bottomless pit of curiosity. What about any other relatives? Did Mother have any others that you knew?"

Norma Jeane nods slowly. "One. I knew Mother's brother's wife, my Aunt Olive. One time Aunt Olive made me two white batiste blouses with handwork. She's still in L.A. But I never knew her husband, my uncle, Marion Monroe. He disappeared. And I wasn't close to my cousins."

"Cousins?"

"Aunt Olive's three children. Betty and Ida Mae and John—but they called him Jack, too."

"Paris," Norma Jeane says, changing the subject, "you really must consider going into the merchant marine." Norma Jeane is effusive as she pleads her case. "You could go where Jim is. We could all be together!"

To Berniece, Norma Jeane adds, "If Paris goes into the service, he must get into the merchant marine like Jim! We could be stationed somewhere together. Wouldn't that be just wonderful! Do you think we can get Paris to do it?"

While Paris sits inside the Pontiac and watches the Saturday afternoon crowds, the "girls"—Norma Jeane, Berniece, Niobe, and Mona Rae—stroll through a fabric store. Berniece's errand is to buy two spools of brown thread.

Berniece pauses next to Norma Jeane, who is dreamily stroking a length of powder blue rayon. "It really does feel a lot like silk," Norma Jeane says softly. Berniece nods. Even rayon is beyond their budgets. Like so many other women in the country, they have become experts in the wartime custom of simulating silk stockings by drawing lines with a dark brown eyebrow pencil down the backs of their naked legs.

"Jimmy likes me with blue near my eyes," muses Norma Jeane, continuing to caress the fabric.

"You're starting to miss Jim more, aren't you?" Berniece holds Norma Jeane's arm and pats her, the twenty-five-year-old big sister comforting the eighteen-year-old bride of two years.

"No! I've been too busy!" responds Norma Jeane. "My mind has been on just enjoying being here with you." She tilts her head and smiles. "Well, yes," she confesses. "I guess I'm starting to miss him. But I'll just have to put up with it."

"You'll be so busy when you get back, you won't have time to notice," says Niobe with a deliberate cheerfulness. "Norma Jeane, why don't you do some more modeling?"

"Well," she nods, "that is on my mind."

"I'll bet what's-his-name will call you to pose again. Daniel? You know, the one who took your picture when you were working in the factory."

"David. David Conover. Yes, he's the one who has gotten me interested."

Norma Jeane reluctantly lets go of the blue rayon. "Yes, I can see about modeling some more." Her voice grows louder. "I'll just put up with missing Jim. A lot of other wives are alone. We're all in the same boat. We'll survive. Berniece, you're awfully lucky to have Paris. He's so nice. And so good looking. Black hair—that's my favorite, dark hair for a man! But isn't Paris going to *have* to go into the service *sometime*? Sooner or later?"

Berniece pushes fear to the back of her mind and answers matter of factly. "He's been deferred so far because he's married and has a child. But, yes, he's expecting to be called. We keep expecting it."

Indeed, the next year Paris was called. He went for his examination, but he was turned down, classified 4F because of previous surgery. In 1945, duty to country was not questioned. So when he learned he could not join up, his relief was mixed with sadness.

Berniece now turns to the fabric store salesclerk, deciding to buy, in addition to the two spools of brown thread, a pattern she has been pondering for several weeks.

"What size, ma'am?" asks the salesclerk.

"Fourteen." Berniece is acutally a size twelve, the same as her sister, but for a sewing pattern she needs a size larger.

Norma Jeane's worries blow away in the explosion of her laughter at Mona Rae's shriek, "Fourteen! Mother, you know you are not fourteen years old!"

Grace wires from Chicago, where Western Union has tracked her down—she and Doc are away from Huntington on another business trip—saying that she has heard from Aunt Ana who had a wire from Jim that he is sailing home for an unexpected leave. Berniece, Paris, and Niobe fly into a dither helping Norma Jeane pack, wanting her to have a glance at Chicago and Huntington before returning to California.

Norma Jeane sends a postcard on October 28 telling Berniece how she enjoyed meeting her and thanking her for the visit. She closes with, "Berniece, I will write to you soon." Not long after, she sends a brief note from Chicago, saying she is on her way to Huntington with the Goddards. She says, "I certainly do miss you, honey . . . You were everything I had expected you to be and even more!' She plans to consult Doc about what Paris should do, still trying to recruit him into the merchant marine or persuade him to look for a job in California. She closes with, "I love you dearly. I always shall, my own dear sister."

Part Two

"Come Out to Los Angeles"

Chapter Eight

A *few months after Norma Jeane's visit to us in Detroit,*
we moved to Oak Ridge, Tennessee. The Tennessee
Eastman Company offered many good opportunities, and it was
closer to Pineville, Kentucky, which we still considered our real
home. The unique advantage that probably cinched the decision was
being able to rent our own house—one of those cute prefab lookalikes
called "Oak Ridge houses."

On March 2, 1945, Norma Jeane sends a short note thanking
Berniece for the "hankies" she'd sent as a gift. Norma Jeane
continues to campaign for a move to California for the Miracle
family, saying, "I hope and pray you will be able to move out here
in California because I know you both would like it once you
move out here, and Berniece I would love to have you near me."
She says Jim has been home about three weeks and they recently
made a trip up to Big Bear Lake, a local resort.

Jim disapproves of Norma Jeane's attempts to build a career.
After a year and a half of determined forbearance, he judges
modeling to be a very expensive hobby. Norma Jeane's earnings
do not keep up with her expenses. She has gone through
their savings, used his allotment money primarily for clothes,
and has even pawned their silverware. Jim is disturbed by her
preoccupation with her career, perceiving that, due to his long
absences, it has replaced him as the center of her thoughts. On
leave during the summer of 1945, he discusses their conflicting
goals.

On June 4, after Jim has been gone two weeks, Norma Jeane
sends Berniece a short letter to let her know that she is staying
with Aunt Ana and pursuing her modeling opportunities. Gladys
will soon be released from the mental institution, and Norma
Jeane is thrilled at their mother's progress. She continues to urge
Berniece to consider a move to California: "I think of you so

much and wish we could be together at least where we could see one another often, for dear I do love you very dearly."

We were barely settled in Oak Ridge when miracles began to happen. For the world, the miracle was that the war ended in August 1945. My personal miracle happened shortly before that. My mother was finally released. She was allowed to leave Agnews State Hospital under the condition that she spend a year with her Aunt Dora Graham in Oregon, so she could have a smooth adjustment period. Aunt Dora began sending me progress reports on Mother.

Dora writes that Gladys seems narrowly focused on a single tenet of the Christian Science philosophy and is intent on trying to cure sick people without the aid of medicine. Gladys has begun to dress in white as if she were a nurse: white uniform, white stockings, white shoes. She first takes short term jobs near Dora, then accepts jobs farther and farther away. Her work also branches out into housekeeping chores and attending to the nonmedical needs of convalescents and invalids. Dora tries, unsuccessfully, to channel Gladys's manic energy into a course in practical nursing.

On July 21, Norma Jeane writes, telling Berniece not to worry about their mother working. "I've talked it over with Aunt Ana and she thinks it might help Mother in this way, that she is doing what she wants to do and keeping busy."

Along with the letter, Norma Jeane sends lipstick and rouge and advises Berniece to get a good lipstick brush. She has consulted with Fred De Liden, Anatole's head makeup man, to get her the right colors. "The lip rouge and cheek rouge were each $2.50, but they will last you a couple of years, so it isn't really expensive in the long run do you think?"

Norma Jeane adds that she misses Jim, that in his last letters, he said he was leaving India and going to Africa. She signs the letter "Your Sister."

Ana writes Berniece, urging constantly that the family get together; Paris and Berniece must come to Los Angeles for a visit, especially since Gladys is out of the institution and can be on her own in a year. Berniece writes to an old friend of Gladys's to check out possibilities of getting Paris a job in Los Angeles. The reply yields no leads.

Just prior to Jim's Christmas leave, Emmeline Snively calls Norma Jeane with the possibility of a modeling job with photographer Andre De Deines, who plans to travel up to Washington State to do a series in western settings. Norma Jeane does not want to go. But the two-hundred dollar salary, relates Jim in his memoir, is exactly the amount needed to repair the burnedout motor in his 1935 Ford, so they decide that she will accept the job. Jim and Aunt Ana, having Christmas dinner alone together, receive a telephone call from a weeping Norma Jeane. She misses Jim and wants to come home. De Deines's photography equipment has been stolen because she left his car unlocked. Feeling responsible for the theft, she sticks it out two more days, finishes, gets paid. De Deines drops her off without coming to the door, and Norma Jeane tells Jim she never wants to work with De Deines again.

Norma Jeane does not, however, decide to give up modeling, and Jim is unable to promise a foreseeable exit from the merchant marine. They reach a highly emotional stalemate in January 1946, and Norma Jeane decides to file for divorce. Emmeline Snively has told her that movie studios are reluctant to hire married women for fear they will get pregnant and quit, resulting in a loss of investment for the studio. Now, with Norma Jeane about to become single again, Snively recommends her to agent Helen Ainsworth of National Concert Artists Corporation, who assigns her to her associate Harry Lipton. Among Norma Jeane's credits by this time are covers for *Laff, Peek, See,* and *U.S. Camera,* and a gossip column notes that Howard Hughes has shown a lively response to one of her covers. Norma Jeane is sent to be interviewed by Ben Lyon of Twentieth Century-Fox. Lyon arranges a screen test, and after studio head Darryl Zanuck sees it, he gives Lyon the go ahead to offer her a contract. In August 1946, under a seven-year contract with six month option clauses, Norma Jeane begins at Fox with a salary of seventy five dollars a week.

Suddenly Gladys is not at Aunt Dora Graham's in Oregon but in Los Angeles. She has flown Aunt Dora's coop before the end of the prescribed year. But Aunt Ana casts her own gentle web of influence, giving Gladys a room in her house and helping her get a job in a department store.

Abruptly, Berniece ends the years of waiting to see her mother. Wishing is out; action is in. In the summer of 1946 Berniece withdraws her savings from the bank and makes ready to fly across the country. Their budget does not permit vacations of any sort. Since years may pass before there is enough money for another cross country trip, Paris and Berniece agree to Ana's suggestion of a three-month get-acquainted visit. Paris, however, must remain at his job in Oak Ridge, and Berniece must take Mona Rae with her.

The upholstery of the airplane seat grows prickly against the backs of Berniece's thighs on this long flight west. Finally they step from the plane in Burbank. Across the tarmac they see Norma Jeane in a cluster of three other women. She is waving one hand wildly; with the other she holds her hair away from her eyes in the whipping wind. Next to Norma Jeane the lively Grace bobs on tiptoes. Berniece guesses at the identity of a large woman with white hair; it can only be Ana. And Ana's arm encircles the stiff shoulders of a petite woman in her mid-forties. With her eyes in slits against the sun and the wind, the small woman stands with arms extended downward into a rigid V, motionless except for her short curls, which are flying like spilled salt and pepper.

Grace and the large woman, Ana, smile broadly. Norma Jeane breaks away and runs to embrace Berniece. She bends and hugs Mona Rae, who exclaims, "Aunt Norma Jeane, your hair is blond now!" They walk rapidly toward Gladys and Grace and Ana.

Norma Jeane carols, "Well, Mother, here is Berniece. And this is Mona Rae."

Berniece is beaming. She squeezes her arms tightly around the petite woman's shoulders, her cheek resting against the tousled gray curls. Gladys places her arms loosely about Bernice's waist for a moment. Then she bends to the child, hugs her, and pats her back.

The group turns and heads for the luggage claim area, arm in arm against the gusts of wind. Berniece smiles brightly—despite the memory stirring of a child on a windy bridge.

Chapter Nine

"How now, brown cow? How. Now. Brown. Cow" Norma Jeane mouths to the mirror in Aunt Ana's hallway. Her lips are rounded as if to blow smoke rings. She stretches out each vowel: "Haahoh naahoh, braahohnn caaahoh."

"That is so ridiculous!" mutters Gladys. "You sound silly. You ought to be doing something worthwhile." Gladys's gray curls bounce in time with her scolding words. "If you don't have anything else to do you can come out here and help me dry clean clothes."

"Mother, I have to improve my enunciation and my vowels," Norma Jeane replies softly. She attends classes at the studio—drama, dance, music, speech—and at home she repeats all the exercises, practices faithfully, and works at improving her diction daily.

"Well, I have to improve these dirty blouses," mumbles Gladys, stamping down the hall and clomping down the backstairs, "because I can't afford to pay the dry cleaners."

Disheartened, Norma Jeane sighs, her gaze falling to the chest beneath the mirror. She presses her lips together and moves her forefinger across the polished surface of the chest in a pacing motion, left, right, left, right.

Berniece thinks: Well, that's terrible. Why doesn't Mother encourage her? Norma Jeane is right at the beginning of a career.

Berniece strides down the hall and stands with one hand on her hip, her head tilted quizzically, watching Gladys.

Gladys is seated on the stoop beside the garage, savagely sloshing a blouse in a pail of cleaning fluid.

"Mother, you ought to encourage Norma Jeane. She's trying so hard to make a go of it. And you're being so ugly about it."

47

Gladys looks over her shoulder at Berniece and mutters under her breath.

"What did you say, Mother?"

"I said I don't like her business."

Norma Jeane has already expressed to Berniece her dismay at Gladys's attitude. "I keep telling myself," Norma Jeane has confided, "that Mother will act better when she has been on the outside longer. I still feel as if we're strangers. I'm still trying to get acquainted with her. When I went to see her in Portland, I felt so . . . lost."

"You mean when Aunt Dora first took her out of the institution?"

"Yes. I drove up there thinking it was going to be one of the most joyful times in the world. Except for seeing her that once in the institution, I hadn't seen her since I was about nine years old. All those years I had waited and wished . . . but when I saw her, she wasn't loving or understanding. She was cold. I felt so let down. Unloved."

Berniece hugs Norma Jeane, a tight, long hug. "I know how you feel, honey."

"We just have to be patient."

Berniece can see that Gladys is going to sulk and so leaves her to herself. Gladys prefers sulking to talking. Whenever anyone asks what she is doing at her job downtown, her reply is abrupt: "Putting tags on clothes." Ana has helped her to get this job, but Gladys is not interested in it and perhaps not doing it too well, for soon she is dismissed. When Gladys is at home, she sits quietly or reads or occupies herself with her washing. Blouses and wool skirts swing from the clothesline nearly every day.

All of Gladys's reading concerns her one and only genuine interest—the Christian Science religion. Since Ana introduced her to it in the institution, she has become obsessed with discovering the possibilities of mind over illness, and she has studied devotedly. Now in the outside world, she has the pleasure of attending Sunday services.

Ana takes the whole group to the Christian Science church each Sunday—Gladys and Norma Jeane, and now Berniece and

Mona Rae. Ana coaches Norma Jeane again, as she had prior
to Norma Jeane's marriage to Jim, reading to her nightly from
Science and Health as the two of them lie in their twin beds in
Ana's bedroom. Ana is immensely likable, nearly irresistible as a
witness for the faith. She doesn't preach; she simply radiates good
nature and optimism.

Berniece and Mona Rae sleep downstairs in the same room
with Gladys, yet the child rarely approaches Gladys. Gladys's
stiffness and emotional distance make her very different from the
child's conception of "grandmothers," and so she doesn't know
what to call Gladys. Norma Jeane suggests Mamacita, Spanish for
"little mother." Gladys finds this suggestion appealing because she
was born in Mexico. Yes, decides Gladys, she definitely likes this
unique name. Clipping it slightly, both Mona Rae and Berniece
begin to address Gladys as "Mamita." Soon it feels natural.

*Aunt Ana and I got along very well. She trusted me and felt she
could confide in me. She told me a lot about her life and history.*

*Aunt Ana's exhusband had developed a drinking problem,
and they hadn't gotten along. When they divorced, as part of the
settlement, she got two houses on the block where we were living
with her. We lived in one of them, and she rented the one next door.
In ours, she also had one room upstairs rented to a man. Mamita's
apartment was one big room on the ground floor next to the three
garages, and Norma Jeane was Aunt Ana's roommate upstairs where
the rest of the living areas were. Aunt Ana had also owned another
house, the one in Van Nuys, which she had deeded to Grace and Doc.
They were at that time in the process of enlarging it.*

*Not only had Aunt Ana befriended Grace and Grace's husband,
but also Grace's best friend's child—Norma Jeane, and then Grace's
best friend—my mother. In addition, she had invited me and my
daughter to stay several months in her house. It was beyond anything
I had ever expected in the realm of friendship. Norma Jeane had told
me that if I ever met Ana, I would love her.*

Ana's is a working household. Ana herself is the first person
outdoors each morning. She cleans the sidewalk covered with
overripe figs that have fallen during the night, zigzagging the

blast from a garden hose across it. Having cleared a path to her car, Ana sets off on her practitioner's duties. The salesman roomer begins his calls; Gladys pins tags through the day; and Norma Jeane either models on assignments for Emmeline Snively's Blue Book Modeling Agency or attends her classes at Fox. In the alley beside the garages, Mona Rae has set up a playhouse. Berniece feels that the visit is going as well as she had hoped, and she plans a visit to the school board to enroll Mona Rae in second grade.

Although there is a small dining room, there are no formal meals at home. At their individual convenience, they eat cereal, sandwiches—easy things. On many evenings, they seek an economical restaurant, for no one seems to have enough energy left to play chef for the household.

One of our dinners out is captured in a photograph of us at a Chinese restaurant. There were three generations of us: Mamita, Norma Jeane and I, and Mona Rae. And there were also Grace and her sister Enid Knebelkamp. Aunt Ana even represented a fourth generation.

At restaurants, Ana helps Berniece and Norma Jeane dodge the young bucks who pursue them, always good naturedly.

Everywhere we went, Norma Jeane and I were stared at. There were always "wolves" around. Norma Jeane was waiting out her final divorce decree, but she still loved Jim. She wasn't serious about anybody else. In fact she had only one date during the months we were there and that was arranged by Fox; she went out with a good looking young actor the studio wanted her to be seen with.

"They want me to date Johnny Sands," Norma Jeane tells Berniece. "I've gone out with him a few times, and they want me to be seen with him tonight."

"Well, by all means, go ahead and go and have fun," coaxes Berniece. "Did you have a good time before?"

"Oh, sure, he's nice. I haven't enjoyed it too much, because it's just to advertise myself. It's a duty usually."

"A duty?"

"Well, it's nice being seen and photographed . . . but parties don't interest me."

"You mean being with lots of people? Drinking? Dancing? That kind of thing?"

"Mmm . . . yes and no," muses Norma Jeane. "Those can be fun things. It's when I have to . . . to get into a conversation with people I don't really know that I get uncomfortable. Not with Johnny. Not with my dates. But sometimes I'd just rather be at home."

"Do you get bored? I can't stand small talk myself."

"Yes, that's what I'm trying to say. Ugh, I hate it. I want people to be impressed with me, but I don't want to have to set out to impress them. Does that make any sense?"

"Sure! I know exactly what you mean," declares Berniece.

"And Johnny, he probably feels that a date with me is work, too!" Norma Jeane laughs.

Johnny arrives and arranges himself on the piano bench, smiling and trim in a tan suit. Berniece wonders if he feels resentful or impatient about the coming evening. If so, he camouflages it graciously. Berniece returns his smile and asks for his autograph. Norma Jeane kids him about giving Frank Sinatra competition as a new popular idol.

51

When Norma Jeane has time off and on weekends, she takes Gladys, Berniece, and Mona Rae for drives. They tour Los Angeles and roam the countryside and the canyons. Among their visits are Chinatown; Beverly Hills (where they wonder if it is really Betty Grable they have spied on her knees digging in a flower bed); Forest Lawn Cemetery with its mesmerizing reproductions of Michelangelo's sculptures; the Farmers' Market; Grauman's Chinese Theater; the Hollywood Bowl. At the beach, between brief dips into the surf, they toss a giant blue plastic ball and play with a friendly collie whose owner says he is one of Lassie's offspring.

Even the ordinary errands interspersed between the sightseeing tours are enjoyable. They chatter nonstop through the Los Angeles streets. "I had a wreck there," says Norma

Jeane. She grasps the steering wheel tightly. Her eyes look ahead while her head points to the side. "Right there. A streetcar and I collided. I was driving in a hurry going from work. It shook me up a little bit."

One of the group's outings has the aura of a trip in a time machine. Grace guides them by Folsom Street near Soto and Euclid in East Los Angeles. As if it has been waiting for this audience, here sits a house built piece by piece by Otis Elmer Monroe, Norma Jeane's and Berniece's grandfather. Then Grace guides them by Highlands Avenue adjacent to the Hollywood Bowl and shows them the house that Gladys had bought and lost. For Berniece the day is so rich with family legacy that it overflows into the night's dreams.

At Grace and Doc's house in Van Nuys they frolic with the Persian cats. Grace and Doc are back from West Virginia, and Doc, without a job at this time, is busying himself doing his own plumbing or puttering with his inventions. With cheerful dispatch Grace throws together a meal for a crowd of nine: Doc and herself, her sister Enid and husband Sam Knebelkamp, Ana, Gladys, Berniece, Mona Rae, and Norma Jeane.

One night in the midst of helping Grace in the kitchen, Berniece and Norma Jeane simultaneously notice the linoleum floor's acoustical possibilities. Instantly the kitchen becomes their stage for an impromptu tap dance duet. They improvise the dance's choreography with only an exchange of glances. Step-shuf-fle-ball-change, Berniece's feet experiment; rattattattattat, echo Norma Jeane's at a slightly faster pace. Knee up. Faster. Kick. Again. Higher. Hand on hip. Hand doffs an imaginary hat. Around. And again. Magic pervades the room as they circle the large kitchen table. They fear that words will make the feeling evaporate. Concluding the routine with delighted laughter, they collapse, breathless. The enchanted moment lingers, durable, almost tangible. The memory endures for both women as the years pass, and it always conjures up a feeling of wonder.

52

N orma Jeane seems addicted to shopping and is saving no money. Dry business matters will become more central in her life, but they occupy small space in her conversations with Berniece this fall of 1946.

Norma Jeane told me that she was supposed to save a percentage of her salary under contract. The Fox contract stipulated that she had to save it. That was standard for minors. Grace had to co-sign the contract for her because Norma Jeane had only just turned twenty in June. As her guardian, Grace was legally in charge of Norma Jeane's finances.

But Norma Jeane spent all her salary anyway and didn't save anything. Looking back, I have to think that her inability to budget was the beginning of her later financial troubles.

In the window of a hat shop, Norma Jeane points to a gray wool tam. "Isn't it pert? Isn't it smart?" she asks. "Let's go in."

Norma Jeane models the hat for Berniece. The gray tam is perched at a rakish angle on the side of her blond head. "I could never have worn a gray hat before I lightened my hair, but this looks great, don't you think?"

The gray tam matches Norma Jeane's gray skirt, and indeed the effect of the sedate gray against the shimmering yellow of her hair is striking. Berniece thinks that on Norma Jeane the hat looks much more chic than on the mannequin head in the window.

"I really want this hat. But I don't know if I could use it or if I should get it. This is the third time I've tried it on," Norma Jeane confesses with a giggle.

Berniece smiles, "If you really want it that badly and it makes you happy, I think you should get it anyway."

Maybe I should have told her to save the money, but I told her to go ahead and get the hat.

She had ordered two cashmere sweaters through the mail, and when they came COD she didn't have the money to pay for them. I gave her the money, about twenty dollars. She said, "I'll give it back to you as soon as I get my check!" I said, "No, let them be my gift. I want to do something for you while I'm here. It'll make me happy."

Norma Jeane had only a very small collection of clothes. She had bought only the best. The main staple in her wardrobe was a light gray wool pencil skirt. She wore it several times a week, with different sweaters and blouses. Norma Jeane always got up early and pressed her skirt before going to work. She said that most of the other starlets came to work in slacks or were sloppily dressed, and some of them wore dirty shoes, or didn't have their hair fixed. They were expecting to get messed up while they were working. But Norma Jeane thought it was very important to look neat from the start.

Norma Jeane said that a VIP at the studio had commented that he was glad to see her come to work looking nice. Her shoes were always repaired and polished. Her hair was always clean and styled and had no dark roots in sight. Regardless of what was scheduled for her at the studio, she went there every single day as neat as a pin. From the very beginning, she was different from the rest of her coworkers in Fox's stable of young actors. Group photographs from those early days show her—even dressed simply in a skirt and blouse—to be the most visually dramatic of them all.

Living with Aunt Norma Jeane is great fun for Mona Rae. Sitting side by side, Mona Rae and Norma jeane play "Chopsticks" on the black Franklin grand piano in Aunt Ana's living room. Mona Rae investigates every nook and cranny of the house.

For Berniece the most exciting adventure is an inside look at the dream factory—Twentieth Century Fox Studios.

"You will have to be an actress today," Norma Jeane tells Berniece. "I've decided on a scheme. You are going to pretend to be an employee and that way we can get you right in."

"Sure!" Berniece agrees. "I'm game!"

Norma Jeane elaborates on her instructions as she drives. "I have to show them my pass at the gate, but you're an employee—a secretary—so you don't have to show the guard anything."

"I don't?"

"While I'm showing him my pass, you just walk right by in a hurry as if you rush in every day and know all about the place."

We were breathless. We were like a couple of teenagers doing something daring. The guard was at the gate. We walked at a brisk trot side by side until we reached the gate. Norma Jeane stopped to fish out her pass, and while she was doing that, I continued walking, as fast as I could go, and then called back, the way she had coached me to do, "Hurry up or we'll be late. They're going to be furious with me." I slowed my pace a little in order for her to catch up. Out of sight of the guard we celebrated our success with a fit of giggles.

We went first to visit a technician, and Norma Jeane scheduled a time for a showing of her screen test. Then she took me by the construction of some new sets going up. And then we freshened up our makeup and proceeded into the office of the casting director, Ben Lyon.

"I'd like you to meet my sister. This is Berniece Miracle. She's here from Tennessee, to visit me."

"I'm so glad to meet you, Mr. Lyon," Berniece says. She hears her own voice, sounding overly loud and rather stiff. "Norma Jeane-Marilyn—has been telling me how you helped her decide on her screen name."

"You two have very interesting resemblances," Lyon comments. His unhurried, confident manner and pleasant deep voice puts Berniece at ease.

Mr. Lyon chatted about names, telling me he was aware that Norma Jeane already had two names taken from the screen since her mother had obviously named her after Norma Talmadge and Jean Harlow. He wanted her to have a shorter name with more flair. Double names sounded too . . . not glamorous enough. After that conversation, it was easier for me to remember to call her Marilyn.

Actually Mr. Lyon had not yet decided on a last name for her, but Marilyn was definitely to be her first name. Mr. Lyon said, "Marilyn likes the sound of Adair. She wanted to be Jean Adair. But perhaps we'll use Monroe. That's a family name and the two M's would be nice."

He was intrigued by my own name, Miracle, and I explained that it is pronounced in Kentucky as if its first syllable rhymes with "tire" and that in Kentucky it is more common than Smith.

He was very pleasant and cordial, and said he was pleased with Marilyn's progress. He said, "Right now Marilyn is very cooperative, but one day she'll probably become like most other movies queens: very demanding." And he laughed.

Stories have a way of surviving if they are the least bit cute or sensational, whether they have any basis in fact or not. It's been said that Marilyn went into Ben Lyon's office for the signing of her contract and the changing of her name all in the same visit. And that Ben Lyon—because the studio personnel department frowned on giving salary advances—personally loaned her fifteen dollars to pay her rent at the Studio Club. Judging by the congenial personality he showed to me, he probably would have been glad to make a loan, but the fact is this: when Marilyn got her first contract, she was living with Ana Lower.

I felt like an executive to be treated to a private showing of Marilyn's screen test. She really went out on a limb to arrange that for me. But she enjoyed watching it as much as I did! She never took her eyes off the screen, and she kept up a running commentary on each movement she made.

The screen test stayed in my mind for days. It seemed to me that Marilyn had taken common everyday actions and movements and made them exciting with her personality. And the color photography in the test was beautiful—the colors decorating the movie set they used for a background, but especially the colors of Marilyn's face and skin.

Norma Jeane and Berniece's day together at Fox proceeds with lunch at the commissary and a tour of the lot. While Marilyn attends a class, Berniece pretends to study secretarial memos at the commissary table where she and Marilyn have their lunch.

56

She looks over her list of people she has been meeting: Ben Lyon; Al Greenway, makeup artist; and Jerry Webb, test director.

When she sees actor Cornel Wilde, Berniece forgets to concentrate on her pretense of being a secretary. Wilde is taking a break from the filming of *Home Stretch*. Moments later, Berniece succumbs to staring when she runs into Jeanne Crain fresh out of a scene on the set of *Margie*. Inside the blase secretary she is pretending to be lies the heart of a moviegoer. Berniece is typical of the generation that found in the movie houses of the 1940s both escape and ideals. So she forgives Mr. Wilde for being about a foot shorter than she expected.

Berniece's enthusiasm for Los Angeles soars, and she writes Paris again, "Come out to California!" He weighs many possibilities for postwar job opportunities, but California is nearly three thousand miles away, too far from his own mother and father.

Marilyn never ventures out of the house looking less than her best. Appearing freshly pressed and freshly coiffed is no easy task in these days before permanent press fabrics and blow dryers. The tiring finale to Marilyn's nightly beauty ritual is setting her hair. Berniece often keeps her company, watching her dip her rattail comb into a glass of water to dampen each strand of hair and wind it with her fingers into a loose circle. Marilyn sleeps with a head of pin curls protected by a hairnet.

One night Marilyn was exhausted and said, "Do you want to roll up my hair for me?" She showed me how, but I didn't get it quite right. The rolls I made were smaller than her usual ones.

We loved to talk about hair and clothes and makeup. Marilyn got a kick out on making up my face for me and showed me how to play down imperfect features and accent good ones. For instance, you could use a darker shade to make cheeks look more hollow, or a lighter shade on a thin lip to make it look fuller. She was an artist with colors on her own face. She told me to be sure and make myself some little eyebrows—draw on a little feather line down each temple where my eyebrows are sparse. She drew those on me, and then did my eyes and my rouge and my lips, and after she finished we went to the mirror and cracked up laughing at the stranger she had turned me into.

Marilyn describes Berniece to her makeup man, and he sends Marilyn home with a box of tiny glass pots with black screw tops, a treasure of custom colors for Berniece. Marilyn continues her instructions, begun in her letters to Berniece during the first flush of her modeling career, revealing the magic tricks of the lipstick brush. "You can't control the line if you apply lipstick with a tube," explains Marilyn. "You can use the brush with ordinary tube lipstick, though, if you want to. And with a brush you can save money because the brush can dig out the last drop. You actually get twice as much lipstick for your money. With the brush you can apply two or three colors for shading. The first step" she continues, "is to outline your lips in a darker color, then shade with a lighter color for contour. All these pots of color can be used for either lipstick or rouge. And watch this—you can even take a tube of lipstick and blend it onto your cheeks and save yourself buying rouge to match."

Like many women, Marilyn and Berniece sometimes discuss their physical defects. "Eyebrow pencil is not just for eyebrows," points out Marilyn. "You can use this pencil to make a beauty mark," she explains, about to demonstrate. Marilyn has a colorless mole near her cheek, a defect that she transforms into a dramatic highlight by painting it dark with an eyebrow pencil. "Some stars even paint them where they don't really have them," Marilyn laughs.

"Why not?" Berniece joins Marilyn in her laughter. "That's not much different from what we did when we drew lines on our bare legs to look like the seams of stockings, is it?"

"I can't put makeup on my hands though, at least not to change the shape" Marilyn moans. "I can't do anything except hide them or turn them at angles. My hands are like duck feet. Big . . . flat . . . webs."

"Marilyn, I feel that way about my blushing. There's no way to hide it" Berniece shakes her head. "And the more embarrassed I get about it, the longer my face stays flushed."

"My ears are worse than my hands," declares Marilyn. "See how thin they are on the tops? Like paper. I never wear my hair pulled back if I can avoid it."

Marilyn continues her list of deformities. The natural beauty of her pre-modeling days has been subjected to trained scrutiny; she is now acutely aware of all her parts and pieces.

"I have a spinal defect or something," Marilyn sighs. "A quarter or half inch of shortness in the bone structure of my left side. It makes me walk funny."

"I think I have that, too." Berniece frowns. "I've noticed that when I have to hem a dress, one side of it has to be turned up a fraction more than the other."

"Really? Stand up and let me look at you. Yes, one shoulder is a little lower that the other. Hold your shoulders back. Now walk. Hmmm . . ."

Marilyn places her palms beneath Berniece's jaw. "Hold your head up, Berniece. You're leaning a little bit forward. Let me show you how they teach us to walk in class."

Marilyn places a book gingerly atop her head, and gives another book to Berniece. The two of them move in slow motion across the living room, successfully balancing the books on their heads. Their shoulders are straight, but their "spinal defects" create inevitable wiggles. They are innocent on this afternoon that wiggles can have commercial value. Up and down Ana's staircase they glide, intent upon holding their necks rigid like steel rods, grimacing to keep from collapsing into gales of laughter.

59

*I*s there any way to draw Gladys out? A key to unlock her capacity to smile and show affection? Gladys's presence had drawn Berniece to Los Angeles, and yet her mother's apathy and gloom are the only dark clouds hovering over these bright days. Berniece stands over Ana's kitchen sink slicing a fig. She fashions a gentle question and continues to hope for intimacy.

"Mamita," Berniece asks casually, "how did it happen that you were born in Mexico?" Berniece has discovered that Gladys is taciturn about the present, but she grows talkative when the subject is her childhood. Stories of Gladys's childhood are full of the family history that Berniece is thirsty for.

"My father and mother lived in Mexico," answers Gladys. "My mother should have come back to the States to give birth to me."

"Maybe they didn't have the money" suggests Berniece.

"They came back anyway after I was born," says Gladys, warming up to her topic, "and we never went back to Mexico. I started school in Los Angeles."

"What did your father do in Mexico?"

Gladys hesitates. Ana smiles and assists the momentum of the conversation. "Your father was working there in Mexico with a paint crew for a railroad outfit, wasn't he, dear?" Ana reminds Gladys of information gleaned from their previous talks when Ana and Norma Jeane visited her in Portland.

"They did all sorts of things," adds Gladys. "Not just painting. He supervised a crew of workers. He was in charge of a crew of quite a few men."

"He was an artist, too," adds Ana. "Art was his hobby. Gladys, dear, show Berniece the painting."

Gladys nods. "This is one of his paintings." She points to the landscape hanging over the couch.

"Berniece, you can have that someday," Gladys decides impulsively.

"So you went through school in Los Angeles?" Berniece encourages.

"I went other places, too. I went to most of the first grade in Missouri where my mother was from. She took me there."

"She left your father?"

"No, she didn't leave him! We were just visiting! She loved him until he died. He was good. My stepfather was the mean one. He threw my kitten against the brick fireplace and killed it."

"Your stepfather . . . uh . . . Grainger?"

"No, no, no, no. Grainger was never my father. My mother didn't marry Grainger until after I was grown. Don't you know that?"

"Well, I . . . uh . . . yes, I knew that." Berniece smiles. "But you mean you had a different stepfather from Grainger when you were little?"

"Yes. My stepfather took us to Oregon and we lived out in the country with his parents. I was nine, ten, maybe eleven. I liked Oregon. I liked his parents a lot, too. They had a farm with pigs. My stepfather was nice, but Mother divorced him because he drank."

"This stepfather is not Grainger," nods Berniece, "but the man who threw your cat against the fireplace."

"No! That was Graves who killed my cat. Chitwood was a nice man. Charles Grainger had a son named Elvin . . ."

"Della had four husbands?" Berniece closes her eyes and presses her fingertips lightly against her lips. She has a fleeting notion that she might begin laughing. Or weeping. This conversation is becoming surreal.

"You were just a child when your father—Otis Monroe—died?" Berniece asks.

"Yes."

"How did he die?"

"He died of paint poisoning. He's buried in Whittier. And my mother, too. They are buried side by side in Rose Hill Cemetery out in Whittier."

61

"That must have been hard for your mother, being a widow with two little children."

"My mother had to work. That's how I met your daddy. When we came back from Oregon, he hired my mother to be the manager for his apartments, and we lived in one of them."

"Mamita, how old was Della when she died?" asks Berniece.

"I don't believe in ages," mutters Gladys. "And I wish you'd stop calling her Della."

"Didn't you tell me she was about fifty-one, dear?" coaxes Ana.

"Fifty-one," muses Berniece. "That was pretty young."

"Yes, it was!" asserts Gladys loudly. "She should have known about Science. But she relied on *materia medica*."

"Gladys, dear," says Ana, "didn't you tell me once that your grandmother in Missouri was very unusual? Was she a private detective? Or was it a real estate agent? Why don't you see if you can remember some of the things about that grandmother, and we can talk tomorrow."

"Berniece, if you had just come a little sooner," says Marilyn wistfully, "you could have met Jimmy. When he was on leave, he came over to get his record player and some things. Darn it, I wish he hadn't taken it. I'm glad this divorce will soon be over, but I still wish you could have met him."

Marilyn speaks frequently of Jim Dougherty, and with affection. She seems to feel no malice in the divorce action; they have simply grown to have opposing lifestyles.

California divorces took a year or more and were very complicated, so to get her divorce Marilyn had established residence in Las Vegas in the spring of 1946. She didn't really move to Las Vegas; she used the address of a friend of Aunt Ana's who lived there. She set her legal business rolling in Las Vegas and came right back to L.A. to do modeling jobs. The process stretched out for longer than the required six-week residency because Jim delayed signing the papers. But finally he accepted the situation and signed them and the day arrived when the divorce was final. Marilyn sailed through

the door on September 13 and gave me a big bear hug and squealed,
"I'm a free woman again! Oh, I feel like celebrating!"

At an elegant restaurant, Marilyn's family and friends converge
to mark her happy day with her. Sam Knebelkamp, a gentle
balding telephone company supervisor, and his wife Enid, who
is a taller, thinner, quieter version of her sister Grace, have joined
the group. Flanking them at the massive table are Grace and Doc
Goddard, Ana, Gladys, Berniece, Mona Rae, and Marilyn.

"Everything really seems to be working out the way you've
hoped," says Sam partway through the meal. "I'm really happy
for you, honey."

"No flies in the ointment, Marilyn?" asks Enid.

"None," smiles Marilyn and emphasizes her reply with a
vigorous shaking of her golden curls.

"What about the problem the other day with your agent?"
asks Doc.

"What was that? Or am I prying?" Sam questions politely.

"Oh, it was nothing," Marilyn answers, her voice up a key. "I
mean, it wasn't anything I shouldn't expect. He was on the phone
with me wanting an increase in his percentage, that's all."

"They got it worked out. It simply means that our girl is
getting more important," pronounces Grace.

"Oh, I feel so good!" Marilyn says. "Things like a little hassle
with an agent are just part of the business. My business. I feel I
really have found what I should be doing."

Marilyn has been granted three wishes this year: a divorce, a
movie contract, and the companionship of her mother and sister.
Although she has denied to Enid the presence of any flies in the
ointment, to Berniece she confides a small misgiving.

With fingertips growing cold against their trumpet top glasses
of CocaCola, Berniece and Marilyn sit in the cafe of Ambassador
Hotel. Marilyn has brought Berniece here to show her Emmeline
Snively's modeling agency. "I have something on my mind I want
you to know about," announces Marilyn.

"What is it, honey?"

"I posed nude for a photographer."

"Really?" The word just drops out and lies limply atop the brief silence that follows. Berniece waits, before deciding how to react further. Marilyn continues.

"I'm not ashamed," Marilyn claims confidently. "I did it. And that's that. But I don't want Aunt Ana to know. She wouldn't approve."

Many other versions of nude photography episodes will hatch in future years, and publicity will vary on reports of Marilyn's motives—from rent to car parts. Reports will also vary on who was the first photographer to shoot her in the nude. But Marilyn doesn't mention the photographer's name to Berniece on this afternoon in 1946.

"Well, maybe Aunt Ana won't see the pictures," Berniece muses optimistically. "Why should she? Would someone show them to her? I really doubt that possibility. What magazine will they be in?"

"I don't know . . . I guess he'll let me know.'" Marilyn arranges her face into a bright smile now. "You're right. I shouldn't worry. She may never see them. I'll decide what to do about it if it ever happens!'"

"Norma Jeane's father was a good looking man like your daddy."

Gladys's words fall out of nowhere. Berniece has made it a point not to upset Gladys by mentioning her father Jasper. What shall she reply? Ana is not nearby to help.

"Jasper was a ladies' man," Gladys continues. "I was walking down the street one day with you and Jackie and saw Jasper coming down the other side of the street with another woman."

Berniece takes a gulp of air and tries to unlock her eyes from Gladys's face.

"He drank too much," Gladys rolls on. "You know that. And he kidnapped you and Jackie and ran off to Kentucky without telling me!" Gladys's face is twisted into a web of angry lines. Her blue eyes seem focused on something many miles past Berniece's face. "How was I supposed to know where he had gone? When I finally found you children, I . . . I had to leave you there. But I used to think I would just go back and live near you and not let anybody know I was there."

Hearing the story from Gladys's perspective for the first time, Berniece feels her stomach winding itself into a knot of sympathy.

"Well, Mamita," Berniece says finally, "all those things are in the past. Let's try to talk about something more pleasant. Did you know that Aunt Ana sent Paris a long, long letter this morning?"

Later Berniece tells Grace about their conversation.

"I think Mamita's starting to open up a little more. She came out with some remarks about Daddy, and about Marilyn's father."

Grace raises her eyebrows in interest, then says, "You know, she married Mortensen because her mother wanted her to. It was her mother's idea."

"I've been thinking . . ." Berniece begins. "Mamita's been through so much . . ."

"Yes, she has. She certainly has!"

Berniece hears her own voice in an uncommonly shrill exclamation. "Just having your children stolen would be enough to drive any woman crazy!"

"Any woman!" echoes Grace. "And yet Gladys held up through the loss of her children. And many other things. There's a lot in her to admire. She's stronger than we realize." Tears shine in Grace's eyes.

"She deserves a lot of credit. I do admire her." Berniece has modulated her voice once more. "I admire her, and I love her. I hope we can eventually feel close to each other."

Grace smiles. "Let's pray for a *complete* healing."

I did want to have time to get through to Mother, but Aunt Ana was the real driving force behind the idea of our making a permanent move to California. She said she would love for us to stay out there and all be together. She said it would be wonderful for Marilyn to have both her mother and her sister. She tried to get Paris to come out and get a job there. But he wrote back saying that he didn't want to be that far away from his people. I loved Los Angeles even more than I had thought I would. But when I was convinced he wouldn't give it a try, I went back to Oak Ridge a little earlier than the three months I had originally planned.

Part Three

"I Would Highhat Everyone *but* My Own Sister . . ."

Chapter Twelve

*I*n February 1947, Florida's booming postwar population grows by another three people as Paris, Berniece, and Mona Rae enjoy their free glasses of orange juice at the state line.

Borrowing three hundred dollars from Paris's mother and hauling a twenty-seven foot trailer by Jeep to Florida, with no job in sight, seems a fearsome gamble. But the decision they made when the Oak Ridge layoffs came has fortunate results. Paris will progress through jobs as a meat cutter and as a paint sprayer and eventually become a counter salesman at Hughes Supply Electrical and Plumbing wholesalers. His starting salary is thirty-five dollars a week.

At the other end of the country, Marilyn's strength is gossamer, like the thread of a spider web that seems fragile but is seven times the strength of steel. It undergoes one of its most severe trials during the period of unemployment that begins when Fox drops her option.

Being dropped was a cause for weeping, but Marilyn didn't give up. She hoped something might come as a result of her two films at Fox, which were scheduled for release the next year. Marilyn had become acquainted with many other young contract players and knew on-again, off-again employment was commonplace in Hollywood.

Berniece receives letters now from the Studio Club, a branch of the YMCA-YWCA, popular housing for many struggling young actresses because it was relatively inexpensive. In the courtyard, they share stories of their ups and downs over noontime sandwiches. But Marilyn prefers work to socializing. She is an incipient workaholic, although at this time she is worried about her economic survival. She accepts whatever assignments Snively and her agent Harry Lipton send her way.

Marilyn told me she was able to keep up her determination through Aunt Ana's love and encouragement. Mother had dropped out of her life again. Our mother did not, as some have written, ask to be taken back into the institution at the end of the summer of 1946. That summer we were all living together. Mother continued working, and after a time she began doing assignments as a practical nurse. She left Ana's and went back to Oregon.

Marilyn takes acting lessons at the Actors Lab, with Morris Carnovsky and his wife Phoebe Brand. In the fall she wins the second lead in a stage production of *Glamour Preferred* at the Bliss Hayden Playhouse. Harry Lipton is pleased with her performance, although the hoped for response from talent scouts does not materialize.

Most histories of Marilyn's career ignore her classes at the Actors Lab and her performances at the playhouse. Her achievements there show that she had stage experience and capacity to sustain a long performance as well as a facility for remembering lines and the power to project her voice to the back of a theater. People who knew her personally were aware of the breathy voice as a gimmick; Jim Dougherty, for instance, comments in his memoir upon this affectation. The whispery voice was Marilyn's creation, along with several other trademarks that combined to produce her public persona.

In February 1948, Marilyn is signed by Columbia at one hundred dollars a week. Her salary is twenty-five dollars more than she had made at Fox, and it is a steady job once more. No longer are her letters daub-by-daub descriptions of makeup techniques. Now they speed through career developments: her studies at the Actors Lab; her appearance in *Glamour Preferred*; her brief movie bits; and bigger movie roles, such as her singing numbers in *Ladies of the Chorus*. At the bottom of one of Berniece's letters to Marilyn, Paris adds a line, a joking backhanded compliment telling Marilyn that he hopes success won't spoil their friendship.

When Marilyn replies, her letter is written on pink stationary imprinted with her new name in blue. Though the letter is written on "Marilyn" stationary, the signature and return address on the envelope read, "Norma Jeane."

"My Dearest Sister," she begins, and says she's started several letters, but can't seem to find the time to finish them. She's in the midst of moving to a new apartment (with room, she says, if Berniece and her family would like to visit) and has just signed a new contract. She says she has a "darling little blond Cocker puppy" to keep her company.

She says she hasn't heard from their mother, "nor do I write her, in fact, all I know is that she is somewhere in Oregon. Where—I have no idea. She and I can't seem to be close due to no one's fault." She wishes things could be different and hopes someday to be of help to her. She goes on to ask about Mona Rae and Paris, answering his comment with, "Please tell him I would high hat everyone but my sister." And she adds a PS.: "Has *Dangerous Years* played down there yet? I'm in it but for heaven's sake don't blink your eyes or you might miss me."

Her handwriting has changed from the sedate vertical strokes of young Norma Jeane to a forward sweeping motion that borders on illegibility. Perhaps the flourish of her racing pen reflects a growing self confidence; in any case, it mirrors the growing momentum of her career.

Berniece and Paris pinch themselves to prove the reality of Marilyn's success. In an Orlando movie theater, they sit delighted with eyes glued to the screen watching for Marilyn to appear in *Scudda Hoo, Scudda Hay*. The blond-haired farm girl in a boat across a lake is almost impossible to spot. Still Marilyn's excitement is only slightly diminished that this is her only scene not cut in the final editing.

Berniece and Paris go see her second film, *Dangerous Years*. As it begins to roll, Paris yawns, "Wake me up when it's over and tell me which scenes they cut out of this one." Berniece's fingernails almost pierce his earlobe when Marilyn appears on screen in a teenage hangout. "Where?" Paris says, as he wakens abruptly.

71

"Oh, with the funny waitress cap." She even has a speaking role this time. "Wow, it *is* her."

Not long after Marilyn's letter, the owner of Palms Trailer Park finds Berniece at the laundry room. "There was a reporter here yesterday asking about you. He left this note. What's this all about?"

Berniece explains that her sister is a movie starlet. "I'm glad you didn't show the reporter where Paris and I live. We don't want any publicity."

A single ripple. No cause for alarm. The trailer park owner, Mr. Mons, has never heard of Marilyn Monroe. He generously offers to get rid of any future uninvited visitors.

The incident seems minor and is almost forgotten.

A second stranger gets rebuffed by Mr. Mons. But following the ripple is another, and another. Marilyn's magazine covers and pinups multiply. Friends begin to appear, clutching magazines in their hands, asking, "Is this her?"

Niobe writes to Berniece from Louisville, Kentucky, stuffing every envelope with clippings, her letters exclaiming effusively, "Toots! Look what I found in a magazine! Looks like Norma Jeane is really beginning to go places."

A crate of clothes arrives from Marilyn. Pinned to the top garment is a note: "To the sweetest dearest sister in the world. NJD." Mona Rae pokes about in the clothes. "Look at this!" she cries, and holds up a gathered skirt covered with tiny stars. 'I think Marilyn wore this in the picture with the lamb!"

A long distance telephone call comes for Berniece through the community pay phone near the trailer park recreation bungalow. Berniece grows mildly nervous calculating the cost as the length of the call grows. As Marilyn rambles on happily, Berniece hears Grace at Marilyn's side tossing in occasional comments. To conclude the conversation, Marilyn makes her way slowly through a report on Gladys.

Gladys is back in L.A. doing housekeeping jobs, which she usually labels practical nursing. Marilyn has her own apartment now, and occasionally picks up Gladys at Aunt Ana's, attempting an evening of conversation. Gladys does not like to sit and chat.

Usually they spend the time doing housecleaning chores together in Marilyn's apartment. Marilyn strains to divert Gladys's urge to argue. "Mother and I could never live together," Marilyn says in a flat tone.

Grace takes the phone and excitedly tells Berniece about the story that she and Marilyn have just invented. "We had to have a biographical story and we had to have one fast! We hadn't dreamed that we would need one, and suddenly things were happening too fast. We made up a story about Marilyn having no parents and being in a lot of foster homes and spending time in an orphanage and Marilyn signed it as being the truth." Their breathless fantasy seems unrestrained by the fact that Gladys is often at Marilyn's side. They know the public loves a rags-to-riches drama.

That story was Grace's idea. She built it around the fact that Marilyn had spent time in an orphanage. Other than that, it wasn't true, but the story served its publicity purpose. And it kept reporters away from Mamita.

Berniece's first twinge of confusion is banished by the pervading excitement of the telephone call. She feels a delicious sense of well being, and she ends her conversation with a declaration that is to become her closing line through future years: "I'm so proud of you. I love you."

The next news from California, however, brings sadness.

A long letter from Grace tells Berniece of Ana's death on March 14, 1948. She says the piano is going into storage and asks if there is anything of Ana's that Berniece would especially like to have. "I'm so very glad Aunt Ana saved the piano for Marilyn," writes Berniece. "I don't want anything. I'm just happy that I got to know her."

At Columbia, Marilyn prepares for a singing role in *Ladies of the Chorus*. She is sent to vocal coach Fred Karger. Karger is divorced, has custody of his child, and lives with his mother. Marilyn delights in romping with Fred's child as well as with his sister's children. The children adore her. She develops a mild crush on Fred, but establishes a solid friendship with Fred's mother Anne, one that lasts throughout Marilyn's lifetime.

73

As Marilyn's list of movie credits grows and she commands larger roles, heavy correspondence and business complexities begin to demand more and more attention. A few years later, following the release of *How to Marry a Millionaire*, an overwhelming seven thousand requests for photographs will pour in each week. As the 1940s become the 1950s, Grace begins to help Marilyn manage her correspondence. Marilyn needs a business filing system, and Grace sets it up for her. The naive pair wonder whether to buy a desk or just a small file cabinet.

Soon telephone calls altogether replace letters from Marilyn. She becomes "a telephone person." Much later, after her death, Mona Rae and Paula Strasberg will discuss this trait. Paula will tell Mona Rae, "I felt writing had some advantages for Marilyn that the telephone didn't. I felt writing would help give her life and her thoughts some organization. I had asked her to write me each Sunday, just as a routine. And she was trying to. It helped bring the random bits and pieces together for her to see them on paper."

Chapter Thirteen

Marilyn rushes from job to job, amassing a hefty number of credits. She tells Berniece that her image in the huge ads for *Ladies of the Chorus*, released in 1948 is locked in her memory with the significance of a "first." More memories pile on, as she watches and analyzes her performances in *Love Happy*, *Ticket to Tomahawk*, *Asphalt Jungle*, *All About Eve*, and *Right Cross*.

At first Marilyn's bit part in *Love Happy* makes the biggest impact. Her role as an anonymous pedestrian is a typical Marx brothers comic bit unrelated to the overall plot. During a chase, Groucho encounters a beautiful blond woman who breathlessly pleads for his help, gasping, "Men keep following me!" Groucho watches her depart and says, "Really? I can't understand why." In June, Marilyn goes on a promotional tour for this movie, traveling across the country by train to New York. Instead of studying the whole *Love Happy* script as she was asked to do, Marilyn carries a volume of *The Actor Prepares* by Stanislavsky. She immerses herself in a study of "The Method," by which actors draw on their emotions and experiences to create realistic characterizations.

Pre-release viewings of *Asphalt Jungle* spark predictions of a high voltage success for the film, and this forecast, combined with Marilyn's accumulation of other credits, enables agent Johnny Hyde to get her a contract with Fox again. In October 1950, Marilyn signs on at a salary of $750 a week, ten times the amount she had made as a starlet when she was let go from Fox three years before.

"Six movies when you didn't have a contract," says Paris, when Marilyn calls with the news. "You don't need one!"

Marilyn says, "Remember that little frog you told me about. About to drown in a bucket of milk. Kicking and kicking until a chunk of butter got churned up and the frog hopped up on it. I guess that's me."

"We don't wonder anymore," says Berniece, "whether you'll stick with it."

A story appears in the media saying that Marilyn was raped as a child. Berniece shudders to think of Gladys's reaction if she should chance upon it. She is grateful that Gladys restricts her reading to Christian Science literature. Berniece explains to an old friend that the stories in the movie magazines never tell the truth about Marilyn's personal life.

Mother sent us a photograph of her new husband, John Stewart Eley, who had come to California from Boise, Idaho. Some months later, after we had moved into our new home, John wrote a long letter to Paris and me saying that he and Gladys wanted to come to Florida to live. John repaired appliances and had a truck outfitted with electrical tools, and his plan was to park his truck in front of our house and make his living working out of his truck. Paris and I wrote back discouraging the idea. After this Grace wrote us and said we had made the right decision. She had found out that John already had a wife in Idaho.

Berniece has earned certification as a bookkeeper, but she must turn down job offers when Hughes Supply transfers Paris to the Gainesville branch as manager of the electrical department. They love the small dream house in Orlando they designed themselves, but they put it on the market and hope that Paris can transfer back after the new branch is running successfully. They wait. And wait.

Paris commutes for a year between Gainesville and Orlando, Mona Rae finishes sixth grade, the house sells, and in June 1951 they rent an apartment in Gainesville. In the fall of 1951 Berniece's father Jasper dies.

Authorities at the Pineville, Kentucky, courthouse are thoroughly confused by the publicity pouring in from the fable mill, and they write to Marilyn asking if she wants to claim an interest in Jasper's property. The local people are delighted to have a reason to write to a movie star, even though they learn from Marilyn's attorney that she makes no claim of interest in Jasper's property.

In 1951 Marilyn was in Hometown Story, As Young As You Feel, Love Nest, Let's Make It Legal. *And the buzzing continued about* Asphalt Jungle *and* All About Eve. *She was studying acting and she felt like she was getting somewhere. But she yearned for more varied roles.*

"I'm happy with the credits I'm building up," Marilyn tells Berniece, "but don't you see a sameness?"

"Paris likes those cute comedies," Berniece says.

"And you?"

"Oh, me too!"

Marilyn laughs. "You're too sweet. Don't you have any criticisms of those one dimensional characters?"

"But you flesh them out so well," says Berniece, and Marilyn laughs again. "No, I mean they're not one dimensional when you play them. And you make them really likable."

"Did you like Angela in *Asphalt Jungle*?" Marilyn asks.

"Well, I felt kind of sorry for her."

"And Miss Casewell in *All About Eve*?"

"Yes, kind of sorry for her, too. You know, people associate you with your magazine covers and the pinups, and they remember those when they see you in movies. So they're just naturally predisposed to like whatever character you play."

"Really? You think so?"

"Yes, I do."

"I'd like to play a character you would hate." Marilyn declares. "I'm going to work toward that!"

By March 1952, the Miracles find that the momentum of Marilyn's publicity has exceeded its similarity to a fast moving train. The launch pad is seared by the blast of the publicity rocket. The secret of the calendars is out.

Paris comes home from work with a roll of a dozen calendars under his arm. His flushed face matches the red velvet background of the nude photographs, for he has laughed his way through an afternoon of ribbing by his coworkers. As a good natured and generous joke, one of them went to Mike's Tobacco and News and bought Paris this supply of calendars.

"Oh, they're beautiful!" exclaims Mona Rae.

Berniece studies each pose carefully. Uppermost in Berniece's mind since the news hit the papers is Marilyn's concern about Aunt Ana's knowing, and how she had said: "I'll decide what to do about it if it ever happens." Now it has happened, and it is indeed having an enormous effect, but not at all the kind they had naively contemplated. Aunt Ana will never know, for death took her several years earlier.

Finally Berniece's eyes leave the calendars, and she speaks. "Both poses look very artistic to me," she decides. "I like them both."

"Good. Let's hang one in the living room then," Paris grins.

"Oh, Paris Miracle, for heaven's sake!"

Personally I did think the calendars were lovely. Marilyn said in show business any publicity is good publicity. But she did have some moments of misgivings herself about the calendars. She asked me to find out how Paris's sister Niobe felt. She said Niobe represented the general public to her. I told her Niobe said she and everybody she ran into was fascinated. She was thrilled to hear it.

78

Most criticism wilts before it can flower, for Marilyn gives a story to news writer Aline Mosby in which she says she posed because she was broke and needed the money. The explanation is perceived as a fitting sequel to the orphan story. The potentially scandalous nude calendar photos help her career rather than hurt it, and Marilyn rides on a tide of popularity that will increase with the successful opening of *Clash by Night*.

Following the calendar uproar, another shocking story broke later that same spring. This second one revealed that Marilyn was not an orphan after all. Marilyn admitted this was true. At least one biographer has written that until 1952 Marilyn permitted the state of California to carry the burden of caring for her mother in a public

*institution. Quite the opposite was true, of course. Mother had been
living in the outside world since 1945 when Marilyn was nineteen.*

In Marilyn's studio press release to Erskine Johnson, she
states that her mother was unknown to her as a child because
her mother had spent many years as an invalid in a state hospital.
At the time of Johnson's article, Gladys had been living outside
for seven years, and had just buried her husband. John Eley died
April 23, 1952. Gladys had already left their rented apartment
and moved in with Grace, and divorce proceedings were well
under way. When Gladys comes to stay with Berniece in Florida
she will refuse to discuss John.

Newsstands overflow with movie magazines featuring
Marilyn and her movies. Friends make sure Berniece doesn't
miss any of them; they discover them all and bring them to her.
Berniece's original scrapbook is squashed in the bottom of a
crate of magazines and newspapers. Articles that perpetuate the
orphan story, adding on more foster homes each year, upset her
and are flung into the trash can.

Marilyn tells Berniece, "Mother still has that idea about
moving to Florida. I can't tell how serious she really is. Grace can
read her much better than I can."

"Well, a change of scene would be good for her. I've mentioned
in letters several times that we'd love to have her visit."

"I'll take care of her travel expenses if she decides. I wish I
had time to come myself. I'd love to relax on the beach with you.
Boy, I wish we had a private beach."

Chapter Fourteen

*F*ive more movies came out in 1952. We're Not Married *and* Monkey Business *were two more cute comedies.* Clash by Night *depressed me. It dealt with limited life choices for women. The critics praised the story as well as the acting. Marilyn was called a forceful actress and a gifted new star. In* Don't Bother to Knock *Marilyn played a psychotic babysitter. It depressed me still more, but I told her I was impressed by her starring role. She was gratified that one of the New York critics had written that she showed "good dramatic promise."*

"It was a challenge I was glad to get," Marilyn tells Berniece. "Did you like the character?"

"Well, I couldn't exactly say . . . well, no."

Marilyn laughs and exclaims, "Wonderful!"

When Paris comes on the line, he says, "I like the comedies. I enjoy relaxing and laughing after a hard week at work. A person needs that. You can't get too much of that."

"That's good to hear," Marilyn says.

Mona Rae tells Marilyn, "My English teacher told my class to be sure and see *O. Henry's Full House* because we were studying short stories. The movie theater gave us a special rate. Do they do that all over the country and beef up box office sales?"

Marilyn laughs in reply, then adds, "I don't know, but what a great idea!"

"Well, people sure wouldn't go to see that Charles Laughton. That is the ugliest man. How could you stand being around him!"

"Who do you think is handsomer, Charles Laughton or Charles Coburn?" Marilyn teases.

"Aaagh! Stop!"

"Okay," says Marilyn. "To answer your question: I wasn't me. I was a person of that era. I like the way period costumes help me become a character. You'll see what I mean if you're in a play sometime at school."

"Would you come and see it?"

"I wish I could come. Listen, hon, how would you like to have a visit from Mamita? She's been telling me she wants to see you and Bemiece."

"Why do you suppose Mother can't make up her mind about coming?" Berniece asks.

"Grace says she's spending hours and hours at the Christian Science reading room. Maybe she'll get things sorted out soon."

Mona Rae, home alone when Gladys telephones to announce that she's in town, recruits a neighbor for a ride to the airport. "I wonder why your grandmother didn't let you know when she would be arriving," he says.

On the way home it is obvious that Gladys is peeved. For several reasons. Death has been speedier in separating her from her husband than the California divorce courts, she is jobless, and she is the mother of a nude calendar girl. It has become Gladys's habit, when she is peeved, to strike back by taking off without letting anyone know.

Berniece and Paris try to entertain Gladys, to play host and tour guide. She remains stiff and silent.

They do find one weekend activity that pleases Gladys, along with the rest of the family—a happy discovery. They take her to swim in Lake Geneva. She likes the fresh water much better than the salty ocean, and she swims and floats to the middle of the lake on her back. But she gets an infection in her ears, a common ailment that Floridians combat with rubbing alcohol. Gladys insists that alcohol is forbidden as *materia medica*. She says that Christian Science will allow her nothing but a hot water bottle to treat it. She complains incessantly of pain in her ears.

"Is Mother helping with anything besides a little bit of cleaning?" Marilyn asks.

"She won't cook at all," says Berniece. "And she has been making long distance phone calls without asking me first. What a shock the bill was! I asked her about it and she said she had forgotten to tell me. Is it forgetfulness or just lack of consideration?"

"Well, maybe it's forgetfulness *and* a lack of consideration," says Marilyn sadly. "I guess she really doesn't, can't . . . you know, I've said that she and I could never live together, and I thought maybe it was just me—just the clash of our personalities—but perhaps, unfortunately, she just isn't cut out to live with anyone. Let's get Mother into an apartment of her own and see if that will work. Can we try it?"

Bemiece feels some guilt for not having good news to give Marilyn about Gladys. Marilyn has more than enough to handle. Her career is blossoming with starring roles. A romance is blossoming with Joe DiMaggio. He had visited her on location during the filming of *Niagara* that summer.

Berniece tries out Marilyn's suggestion, proposing the apartment idea to Gladys. She refuses to discuss it.

After seven weeks of living together, with four people bumping against each other continually in the cramped apartment, Berniece calls Grace on October 30, seeking advice from the friend who has known Gladys best.

"Berniece, I admire you for trying to be optimistic," Grace soothes. "But honey, as I see it, it's impossible. Let's just accept it. Perhaps things will change in the future."

Marilyn agrees with Grace's judgment. Concluding their conference, Marilyn directs Grace to mail Gladys a ticket to come back to Los Angeles by train.

Berniece's relief is mixed with pain. Once again she has missed the mark. She yearns for moments of closeness with her mother, but intimacy continues to elude her.

And as Berniece seeks to form a coherent view of Gladys from countless random outbursts, she will find the courage to ask Gladys an important question.

"Mother," says Berniece, "I'd like to hear about Marilyn's father."

"Marilyn's father was an important man in the movie industry," Gladys answers blandly.

"Isn't . . . wasn't her father Edward Mortensen?" asks Berniece.

"No."

Berniece feels dizzy. A silent hammering of anger begins within her ears. Berniece continues calmly. "Does Marilyn know that?"

"Yes, I told her. Grace told me to tell her."

"When did you tell her?"

"Oh, I don't know. Not too long ago."

"What did Marilyn say? How did she react?"

Gladys purses her lips and shrugs her shoulders.

"Did Marilyn ask you why you hadn't told her before?" Berniece presses.

Gladys stares at Berniece, frowns, stretches the frown away, and frowns again. "I told Marilyn that Grace said we should wait until she was old enough to understand."

"I see." Berniece swallows hard.

"You want to know how it happened!" Gladys snaps, and leans toward Berniece, her angry blue eyes wide in challenge.

Berniece looks down at her folded hands, then back at Gladys.

"If Marilyn wants you to know," Gladys states, "*she* can tell you."

Berniece blinks her eyes, collecting her thoughts. Her cheeks balloon, and a stream of breath flows slowly through her lips.

"All right, Mother, I understand. All of this was long ago in the past. Let's just forget about it."

"I'd like to!"

When Mother got back to California, she went straight to Grace and Doc's house. She started screaming on the front porch about Grace sending a train ticket instead of a plane ticket. Grace said Mother stood there in a rage yelling at them without stopping.

Grace and Doc were afraid to come out. They didn't even open the door because Mother was so wild. They finally had to call the ambulance to come get her.

So, after seven years of freedom, Mother was committed to an institution for the second time. The following spring Marilyn's request for Mother's admission to Rockhaven Sanitarium was approved, and she was transferred there.

Chapter Fifteen

Grace writes Berniece on July 4, 1953:

7:30 a.m.

Dearest Berniece,

I have been up since 5:30 this morning, fixing up an index system for Marilyn so she can keep her bills and messages in order.

Poor little weak sick girl. I suppose you read about her being in the hospital with near bronchial pneumonia. She never has regained her strength. I really mean it when I say that next to President Eisenhower, she is next in line as far as the demands on her time are concerned.

On June the 9th she finally made it out here to go thru eight or ten big cartons of old fan mail (which has been here over a year and she couldn't get answered) and scrapbooks, magazines, etc., etc., etc.

Doc got home about 6:30 and helped her finish.

She took me back to her apartment that night and what a week I spent with her.

I made her stay in her bed as much as I could and I put the phone in the living room, muffled it in pillows so she couldn't hear it ring and I took all messages.

It rang constantly and the front door and back.

[Grace continues with six pages of miscellaneous news, and then the letter addresses her own illness.]

. . . I had to have $75.00 worth of x-rays and florocope examinations before I went. However, I am all right as far as the cancer is concerned, but, I have to have a hysterectomy operation sometime soon and then maybe I'll begin to feel like a human being again.

The night of June 13 (I was at Marilyn's) and we had planned to phone you but as usual something interfered. Her Publicity agent from Fox came up and stayed for several hours having her sign her name to photographs and write some personal notes to very important people. So, by the time he left it was too late to call and the next day you had gone on vacation . . . .

Lovingly,
Grace

The eight page letter is typical of Grace; but she will write no more long letters, for her energy dwindles rapidly. Her death comes three months later on September 23, 1953.

"I feel an anchor is gone." Marilyn tells Berniece.

"I have no doubt. I'm in shock."

"Life is just one loss after another. What will I do without her?"

"Is Joe of some comfort?"

"I guess he's more important than ever to me now," Marilyn affirms.

Marilyn and I discussed many times how sad we were about the circumstances of Grace's death. It's disturbing to see stories say that Marilyn had dropped Grace Goddard because she felt her marriage to Jim was one of convenience engineered by Grace. Marilyn never dropped Grace. Grace was always Marilyn's friend, and Marilyn loved her until she died.

Grace had cancer of the uterus. When Marilyn learned of Grace's death, she thought Doc should have encouraged her to go ahead with the surgery. Perhaps he did. But ultimately it is a person's own decision. Nevertheless, Grace's death seemed terribly sad and needless to Marilyn and me and we never really got over it.

Doc allowed Marilyn and me to believe that Grace had died as a result of the cancer. Marilyn never knew the real cause of Grace's death. Nor did I until 1979 when I wrote California for her death certificate. When I saw the official document, I had a far greater shock than the one I felt when I was first told of her death. The cause of death states: suicide by means of barbiturate poisoning; ingestion of phenobarbital. *She was fifty-nine.*

As Marilyn's career grows, her business affairs grow in complexity, and her time to manage them diminishes. She had

85

outgrown Grace and Doc's capacity to help in this area, and following Grace's death, she looks for a business manager. Marilyn hires Inez Melson. Inez will impress Marilyn with her stability, and even after Inez tells her, "You've gotten too big for me," Marilyn will continue to rely on Inez for counsel.

In December, bolstered by courage derived from Joe, Marilyn walks out of a production of *Pink Tights* and a costarring role with Frank Sinatra. She objects to the script, to her lack of director approval, and her salary. She wants a voice in choosing the roles in which she is cast. She feels that the role in *Pink Tights* is not only a demeaning characterization but also poorly written. She has taken the only route available to her to fight the studio heads. In retaliation, Fox places Marilyn on suspension.

Marilyn lacked the confidence to deal with the studio alone. And she mistrusted the intentions of many people who surrounded her at that time. Her thoughts were enough to keep anybody awake at night. She tried to picture what would happen in the future when she married Joe. And what might happen if she committed herself to Milton Greene's plans for a production company. The loss of Grace made Joe rather precious. She saw him as a rare, trustworthy friend.

86

"Wooo! Wooo!" cries Niobe. "Jane Russell, Betty Grable—the big ones, honey. Marilyn's up there with the big ones."

"And they're nice people, too, she says, great to work with," Berniece replies.

It is 1953 and they have seen *Niagara*, a drama of passion and intrigue, which people were flocking to see. This is followed by the release of the two comedies that have Niobe so excited: *Gentlemen Prefer Blondes* and *How to Marry a Millionaire*.

"So, tell me," asks Niobe, "why in the world has she walked out when she's right on top?"

"She isn't getting to do the kind of roles she wants to do. From her point of view, she isn't on top at all."

A box of clothes arrives. Mona Rae tries on an emerald green two piece shirred swimsuit that Marilyn wore in a pinup. "Don't tell anybody where I got this," Mona Rae warns. "I don't want anybody comparing me with Marilyn!"

Also in the box is Marilyn's wedding gown. It seems that Marilyn is sweeping away the last remnants of her time with Jim Dougherty. A marriage to Joe DiMaggio is definitely in the offing.

Berniece converts the old white lace wedding gown into a ballerina length party dress for Mona Rae (instinctively saving every swatch of fabric for future restoration), and Mona Rae wears the dress on her first date in the fall of 1953.

The next time Marilyn calls, Mona Rae's first question is unadorned by tact: "Are you going to marry Joe DiMaggio?"

Having met in the spring of 1952, Marilyn and Joe have made headlines as a romantic pair for about a year and a half. The public loves the match between these two poor kids who grew up to become a baseball hero and America's favorite blond. They will marry within a few weeks. Mona Rae smiles, hearing Marilyn's soprano laugh. "He's the only man in my life," comes the purr over the telephone. "I love him very much."

"Well, you make a *darling* couple," pronounces Mona Rae.

Marilyn marries Joe DiMaggio on January 14, 1954, at San Francisco City Hall. Their few guests are Joe's friends and family. A ballpark assemblage of reporters waits outside. Marilyn and Joe's happiness will not thrive in the glare of publicity, and before the year is out, Marilyn files for divorce. Again a crew of photographers descends, swarming over the car where she is trying to cover her tears.

While her 1954 releases were playing in the theaters, Marilyn was in New York finalizing arrangements for a partnership with Milton Greene to form Marilyn Monroe Productions and making The Seven Year Itch. *Her life was changing. The films that came out in 1954 were* River of No Return, *a western, and* There's No Business Like Show Business, *a film tribute to Irving Berlin. But what got the most publicity was the making of* The Seven Year Itch. *Joe was unhappy, to put it mildly, watching the photographers and cameramen endlessly shooting Marilyn's dress flying up. Behind the hoopla was* the simple fact her career consumed too much of her time—time Joe felt belonged to him. We had been as excited over their marriage as over any films Marilyn had made. We were so sad for her.

Mona tells Berniece, "When I sat there during that 'Heat Wave' number in *Show Business*, the sweat was pouring off me. Not from the heat, though, from embarrassment. When she started caressing the trees and wiggling everything including her upper lip—well, the kids from school were screaming and whistling. I sort of see Joe's viewpoint."

"What I see is another loss for Marilyn," Berniece replies. "She wants to play other roles."

Most people thought that Marilyn was playing herself in roles like she had in Show Business, Monkey Business, *or* Gentlemen Prefer Blondes. *Viewers based this opinion upon the seeming lack of skill that her roles required and upon the similarity between these characters and the public image she projected during the first half of her career.*

However, most of the roles that were given to Marilyn were the opposite of her personality. Marilyn was not a dumb blond. She was thoughtful and determined and a workaholic. She insisted on perfection from herself in her scenes. Her insistence frustrated several of her directors who were happy with the first take and had to suffer through dozens more at her request. On the set, Marilyn was her own slave driver. Off the set, over her lifetime, she allowed herself very few vacations. She appeared where she had to appear at the request of the studio, but she was not a social butterfly and stayed too busy to do much dating. Although she left high school after the eleventh grade, and although there were gaps in her general knowledge, she had a good academic record and throughout her life was a voracious reader. Marilyn's constant reading only seemed to earn her criticism and ridicule. The real Marilyn was thought to be the phony one.

"I still feel I'm doing what I'm supposed to be doing," Marilyn tells Berniece.

"It seems such a tough business. I can't help wondering if it's all worth it."

"Well, some changes are around the corner."

When Marilyn said she was doing what she was supposed to be doing, she meant show business felt like her proper destiny. I had heard her say it before, and I would hear her say it again.

At the end of our telephone calls, I always told Marilyn I was proud of her and that I loved her. And so often she would repeat to me as we said goodbye, "Please promise me you won't give out stories about me." And I would always say, "I promise." I had vowed to myself that I would never be a troublesome relative. I wanted to do exactly as she asked. She resented it very much when Jim's sister gave a story to the press. She never got over that resentment.

Later on she warned Paris and me that steering clear of publicity for ourselves was the only way to have a normal life. We wanted a normal life, and she wanted a normal life for us. She knew what it was like—she suffered from having to live twenty-four hours a day in a fishbowl and hoped to protect us from that.

I understood what she meant. I never complained to her—not once—but the work of avoiding reporters had already placed our lives outside the range of "normal," and there were no signs of it slowing down.

Mona Rae, in her early teens, is angry and resentful at the impudence of strangers who encroach on the joy of having sweet Norma Jeane as an aunt. But the young girl develops a method that Paris has already mastered. Kidded constantly at his office, he uses humor as his armor. As Mona Rae continues to build a shell against curiosity seekers and suspects the motives of people she doesn't know, she cultivates a friendly smile and a ready joke as her standard reply. "Oh, no, you're mixed up," she will grin. "Elizabeth Taylor is my aunt." Or she may say, "You're talking to the wrong person. Follow that girl who just went in the drug store!"

In the spring of 1954, Paris and Berniece move from their apartment to a house on the opposite side of town. Stalking reporters follow. A persistent reporter from *Time* magazine sleeps all night on the cold concrete of the front porch, and as Paris steps over him on his way to work, he asks, "Have a good night's sleep, buddy?"

Chapter Sixteen

*B*erniece's annual trips to Kentucky have always included a visit to her stepmother Maggie. Shortly after her yearly visit in September 1955, Maggie dies quietly in her sleep in Flat Lick at the age of eighty-two. Found pinned to Maggie's underclothes is an envelope of money she has saved for her funeral and a note to Berniece explaining the arrangements she prefers.

Contributing to the drain on Berniece's emotions is her concern for Marilyn as she sees her new business venture grow in complexity. Forming her own production company had caused a flurry of legal activity at Fox that eventually ended with a much better contract for Marilyn. And she had just arranged to produce *The Prince and the Showgirl*, in which she would star with Laurence Olivier.

In New York, Marilyn employs the Arthur Jacobs agency to handle her press relations. Lois Weber is assigned to her, to assist in a slowdown in publicity—the first time Marilyn has found it necessary to make such a decision. During this year Marilyn's awareness of the press's potential as an enemy first surfaces in full strength. The press has helped make her famous; it has given her the exposure that built her career; it has been a friend. Now articles appear criticizing her attempts to change the direction of her career.

To Marilyn, it seems that the public is both confused and angered by her refusal to conform to the dumb blond image it holds of her. She recognizes that she set the process in motion with her first decision to create a fantasy image. Now she perceives the media's power to invade her privacy. Whereas in the past she has warned Berniece to be on guard, wary that public curiosity could result in embarrassment and inconvenience, now Marilyn's concern is evolving into fear. To have one's problems and experiments bathed in the same glaring light as one's triumphs can wither courage.

In New York, Marilyn was overflowing with excitement— explaining her plans and her projects, telling of the artistic people she was meeting, and describing the way Lee Strasberg could help actors use their sensitivity. She had settled on an analyst she liked very much, Dr. Marianne Kris, who lived in the same building as the Strasbergs. Whether she would have begun analysis if she hadn't become involved with the Strasbergs is difficult to say. Lee encouraged it almost as a part of training for his students. He and all his family went for therapy. He felt that whatever helped actors gain insight into their feelings was good.

Marilyn was going through a great many changes. In the space of only one year she had gone through a marriage and a divorce, a temporary break from her studio, and a move to a new city. It took a tremendous chunk of courage and assertiveness to do that, and it took a lot out of her because she was not a self confident person. Determined, yes, but never secure.

Throughout her life Marilyn was attempting to grow. With the move to New York, she felt that she was starting over. Everything was new. She was making new friends. She was optimistic about the plans she had for the company she and Milton Greene had formed. She was thrilled with the encouragement she was getting from Lee. Not only did she get recognition for her talent and the kind of training she wanted, but it was coming from the man she felt was the best in the field.

Psychologists say that too many changes in too short a time are extremely stressful, even if the changes are happy ones like a job promotion or a wedding. So, even while Marilyn was doing what she wanted to do, she felt ill at ease. And although I was glad that she was getting help through analysis, I was just wishing it weren't even necessary.

Mona Rae studies speech and drama, appearing in every dramatic and musical production mounted by her high school. She has become very serious about acting. She comes to admire Marilyn's studies in Los Angeles with Natasha Lytess, her studio coach, and with Michael Chekhov, a former student of Stanislavsky. And she is delighted when Marilyn begins to study with Lee and Paula Strasberg of the Actors Studio in New York, whom she worships as the high priest and priestess of American theater. She is "absolutely thrilled" when Marilyn marries Arthur Miller, America's most distinguished living playwright, and is deeply moved by Marilyn's performance as Cherie in *Bus Stop*, which comes out a few weeks after her marriage to Arthur. Now Mona Rae stands her ground when approached by curious strangers and says with relaxed sophistication, "Yes, we're very proud of her."

When Marilyn and Arthur return from England and the making of The Prince and the *Showgirl* in October 1956, *Bus Stop* is still playing in the theaters. Marilyn is gratified to find it a success. Critical comment is uniformly excellent. But this sense of well being is dashed by another loss. While she and Arthur are living in Amagansett, Long Island, Marilyn is rushed into surgery to terminate a six-week tubal pregnancy.

"My heart is broken," Marilyn tells Berniece.

"I'm so sorry, honey. But you will be all right, won't you?"

"I'll try again."

"Mona Rae and Paris want to talk to you."

"You were wonderful as Cherie," Mona Rae gushes. "I forgot it was you."

"That's the best compliment I could get, Mona Rae," Marilyn sighs. "Really."

Mona Rae graduates in June 1957. She tells Marilyn she has enrolled in Florida State University in Tallahassee and plans to teach high school.

"Talla—which?" stutters Marilyn. "How do you spell that?"

"It's an Indian name," laughs Mona Rae.

"Oh, I'm so glad you're going to be a teacher," says Marilyn. "That's important work. So much more important than acting."

To Berniece, she says, "We're settled now. Why don't you come on up? I can't be a mother just yet, but I'm just being a homemaker for a while. I won't be working. I need to just spend time with Arthur."

"A homemaker?"

"Sure! Hey, you can teach me to make fig pie!"

"Fig pie? What's that?" Berniece is pondering Marilyn's tone, trying to read between the lines to gauge the degree of enthusiasm behind Marilyn's new vocation.

"Remember when we tried to dry figs at Aunt Ana's? You just hated that the figs were going to waste! And you said you were going to invent a recipe . . ."

"I was? What a bunch we were! Remember how you tried to pick out a bathing suit of yours that would fit me, and I leaned over and shook and shook, but I just couldn't quite fill up the cups!"

On Arthur's advice, Marilyn breaks her partnership with Milton Greene, buying him out in the spring of 1957, two years after the company's inception. She continues at the helm of Marilyn Monroe Productions. For the first time in twelve years Marilyn is not involved in film making or in maintaining a fantasy self to face the world. She and Arthur buy a three-hundred acre farm in Roxbury, Connecticut, not far from the site of his former one. Marilyn relaxes by managing its remodeling and decoration. In the late spring she goes into the hospital for gynecological surgery; she will continue to try for another pregnancy. That summer, they acquire a Manhattan apartment in addition to the farm. Marilyn supervises its decoration also, lovingly designing a study for Arthur. They divide their time between the city and the country. Arthur works on a screenplay that will feature Marilyn, a creation that becomes *The Misfits*. Also underway is Norman Rosten's adaptation for the screen of Arthur's play *A View from the Bridge*. May Reis, a secretary who had formerly worked for Arthur alone, is hired to handle correspondence for Marilyn. In spite of Marilyn's not working, there is a massive amount of correspondence as well as offers to attend to. May is steadfastly loyal to Marilyn; without the common lust for gossip, she is one of the few people in whom Marilyn's trust never wavers.

93

Chapter Seventeen

Berniece worries about Marilyn. She grows increasingly uncomfortable whenever she stops to count the months she has had to postpone her visit to New York. She replays a telephone call in her mind, one in which Marilyn's invitation had begun to carry a vague note of urgency.

"Where were you yesterday?" asks Marilyn. "I tried all day to call you."

Berniece laughs self consciously. "I went shopping. And I was playing bridge in the afternoon."

Marilyn teases her. "Oh, what a lady of leisure you are. I wish I had time to play bridge."

"Well, normally, I don't. I'm between jobs. I'm waiting to hear about my interview for a bookkeeping job at the University of Florida."

"I've tried three times today to reach you."

"Gee . . . I'm sorry you missed me. Well, how are you? It's so good to hear your voice."

"Oh, honey, it's soooo good to hear you, too. How am I? Well I'm lying here in bed with a bandage on my hand holding it up in the air to keep it from bleeding. I cut myself trying to slice a ham."

"Is it serious?"

"Oh, no. I'm just an incorrigible klutz. I'm so glad I got you this time. I just had to talk to you. In fact, if you're not working, you ought to come up to see me now. I really need you to be with me. I often think about how you and Paris have been happily married for so long."

After several minutes of conversation, Marilyn says, "Arthur's here. We both want you to come. We've talked about it, and we'll pay your expenses. This is a perfect time. I'm not making a picture and you're not working. When will we ever find such ideal circumstances again? Here, say hello to Arthur. He's here."

"We've found an apartment we're very pleased with," Arthur tells Berniece. "Three bedrooms and a study. Two baths. We'd like very much for you to come visit us. There's plenty of room."

Berniece promises to talk it over with Paris. That evening she tells him of the afternoon's conversation, hoping to work the invitation into other details.

"Ham?" repeats Paris. "You must have heard wrong. Jewish people don't eat ham."

"Well, maybe they're not perfect," Berniece responds. "I'm just telling you what she said."

"Maybe it was just for guests," grins Paris.

"My hearing is fine," Berniece insists, then her tone changes. "I'm glad she thought of me when she hurt herself."

Marilyn and Arthur had moved from the Connecticut farmhouse and were living in their apartment in Manhattan. She said they had already talked at length about my coming up. I was terribly excited and longing to spend some time with her. But I was also afraid of reporters catching me, and I didn't know how to cope with Paris's not wanting me to go on trips by myself. I talked it over with a friend who said I should travel incognito.

A couple of weeks later, while I was still pondering all the pros and cons of an incognito trip, Paris strolled in and announced that he had to go to New York on business for his company. I said, "Oh, good! I'll go with you."

But Paris wouldn't hear of my going. He told me that he and two other employees were going and the wives could not go. I was very upset, but I knew Paris didn't want to be set upon by reporters and have his business trip messed up. I knew his job had to come first; I understood the fear that made him finally end our argument by saying to me, "If you go, I won't." I was miserable, torn between keeping Paris happy and giving Marilyn some support beyond just telephone conversations. Still, I kept remembering how Marilyn had referred several times to my being happily married for so long. She talked about that instead of the usual newsy tidbits. It was becoming apparent that she and Arthur were having problems.

95

But the biggest reason for my resentment was the sheer irony of what Paris and his coworkers did on their trip to New York: they visited Marilyn and Arthur!

Paris went with Robert Peacock and Dan Polar. Paris had called Marilyn during a break from business, using the unlisted number I had given him. He had talked to her secretary and then to Arthur, who invited all three of them over for the evening when Marilyn would be home.

They had been sitting in her living room talking with Arthur for about half an hour when Marilyn arrived. She had been out buying flowers and was two-thirds hidden behind an armful of something that looked like dogwood blossoms.

Marilyn served everyone cocktails, and she kept Paris's friends laughing by forgetting which was which. She called one of them "Mr. Polar Bear" and the other "Mr. Bird." She gave them all photographs; Paris's was signed, "Love & Kisses from your Sister-in-Law." When they got back, Paris entertained his boss with a description of Bob Peacock trying to sneak out with one of Marilyn's highball glasses, which turned out to be too big to fit into his coat.

Later on, predictably, Marilyn was doing a picture and I was working. I was certainly no pioneer in the women's awareness movement, but I think that some seeds of self-assertiveness started to sprout in that fall of 1957.

Marilyn says, "You must see my homemaking efforts, Berniece. Did Paris describe our apartment to you?"

"He said it was beautiful."

"You know that bust of Abraham Lincoln that you told me Paris's dad had gotten somewhere? Well, just wait till you see what we have in the foyer here."

"You're not going to tell me?"

"I just gave you a hint! Now you have to come see in person!"

"Decorating has turned out to be a lot of fun for you, hasn't it?"

"I must have inherited a little bit of our grandfather's artistic talent. You'll be pleased. And I want to show you New York.

When are you coming? Mona's tucked away in college; you're not working yet; are you coming soon?" Marilyn asks.

"I hope to. Paris wants me to travel with him a little."

"Oh that's wonderful. You should!"

At Christmas, Mona Rae got an engagement ring. She transferred back to Gainesville. Then in March, Paris's father Wilbourn died. Two months later, at the end of her freshman year, Mona Rae married. She cherished the gift from Mr. and Mrs. Arthur Miller—a massive silver tray. Two months after that, in July, Marilyn was preparing for another movie.

Marilyn's rest comes to an end when she and Arthur fly to Hollywood in August 1958 for the filming of *Some Like It Hot.* Although her lifestyle as homemaker is interrupted, she has a wonderful secret to keep her happy. She has just learned that she is pregnant.

Marilyn invests the supporting role of Sugar Kane with such vitality and comic appeal that it seems to be a major one, equal in importance to those of Tony Curtis and Jack Lemmon, around whose adventures the major plot revolves. The film is done in black and white because the makeup worn by Curtis and Lemmon to impersonate women would be garish if filmed in color. Initially Marilyn objects to this decision, but ultimately she will concede that it is appropriate and successful. This film is destined to become the most durable hit of her career.

By certain yardsticks, Marilyn now has everything she has striven for. She is married to an artistic, supportive husband. A significant expression of her devotion to him is her conversion to his religion; his gift to her is the investment of his talent in a screenplay for her, which he finishes this year. She has a home in the city and a home in the country. In both, she has created an atmosphere of comfort and love. Not only can she bask in the affection of Arthur's children, but she is also expecting the child she has always wanted.

She is president of her own corporation. She has grown significantly in her ability to draw emotion from audiences through the realism of her performances. Her family is well, her mother safely ensconced in a fine sanitarium, her half sister's

97

family thriving in Florida. Ex-husbands express no animosity, nor does she ever speak of either without dignity. She keeps in touch with a select few friends in California, such as Anne Karger, and she has a circle of loving friends in New York. Not insignificantly, she has a dog, Hugo the bassett hound, who travels back and forth from Roxbury to Manhatttan on each trip, for Marilyn's fondness for dogs is second only to her love of children.

Indeed, Marilyn recognizes that her blessings are many, but a mist of depression hovers. Her confidence in Arthur dropped after she discovered a disturbing journal entry critical of her habits. Knowing that Arthur can become impatient and judgmental makes her tense. During the course of their marriage, Arthur has found himself cast in the role of caretaker and mediator. He has often had to monitor Marilyn's pill consumption and to smooth over its effects upon her career and relationships. Marilyn suffers a miscarriage at three months, in November 1958, directly after finishing the filming of *Some Like It Hot*. She returns to her habit of taking tranquilizers to relax and to sleep, a habit that had been under control while she was pregnant.

Berniece is besieged by telephone calls at all hours, day and night, as reporters pursue her for stories on Marilyn. She gets an unlisted telephone number, yet has to change it frequently. Reporters stalk her at work, too, but her friends and her boss keep her alerted, and she manages to dodge most of the unwanted visitors.

The release of *Some Like It Hot* in March 1959 fires immense acclaim. Berniece congratulates Marilyn, knowing, of course, that she would be much happier to be getting congratulations on the birth of a child.

"I'm so glad Arthur was by my side for the premiere," Marilyn says. "I was scared."

"Oh, you shouldn't have been! Everybody loves it."

"But I was scared," repeats Marilyn, "that I might look fat on screen—showing a little, you know. Then I was afraid I would cry when I thought about losing the baby. But things turned out okay. Seeing Arthur laugh made me feel good."

Berniece tells Marilyn, "All of us have been cracking up over it. It seemed to be much more lively than *The Prince and the Showgirl*. Very lively."

"Is that a compliment?" Marilyn teases.

"Oh, yes!" says Berniece.

Mona Rae, on the extension phone, interrupts to offer her analysis. "Maybe it's the difference between American and British . . ."

"Or between Olivier and Lemmon and Curtis," laughs Marilyn.

"Oh, you were wonderful in *both* films!" exclaims Berniece.

"Mona, honey, I'm so glad you're sticking with college," Marilyn says. "What a hard worker you are, going to school year-round."

A friend of Berniece's tells her, "We thought *Let's Make Love* was a little dull in comparison with some of her others, but a lot of people are seeing it, aren't they? Do you think it's because of all the publicity about her and Yves Montand? I overheard some people near the ticket booth."

"It isn't true," says Berniece. "She is not like that." Berniece is adamant on the point, through the years. She is gratified when poet Norman Rosten later writes that "Marilyn did not get involved with married men. She hated the idea of people sleeping around."

99

I always knew that stories of an affair were based on a series of publicity stunts to boost interest in the movie. It was true, however, that her marriage wasn't working. It was impossible, I concluded, for people in show business to lead normal lives. But the pain, why such pain? Marilyn and Arthur's fairytale marriage evolved into a nightmare of depression for both. Shortly after finishing the filming of The Misfits, *Marilyn flew to Mexico for a divorce.*

"Didn't you once tell me about an actor who had a nervous breakdown because he got so wrapped up in 'The Method'?" Berniece asks, referring to Lee J. Cobb, who played the lead in *Death of a Salesman* for 742 performances.

"Not exactly," explains Mona Rae. "He was, however, so wrapped up in the role of Willie that when he came off stage, he was still in character. Many actors—not just 'Method' actors—find themselves living the role off stage."

Mona Rae pauses a moment in thought. "But I don't think that's Marilyn's problem, identifying with the characters she plays. If that were the case, she'd more likely be a comedienne, letting problems roll off her back. If it's a question of identifying, I think it's more likely she identifies with real people—real actresses."

"You mean, like her telling me she knew how Garbo must feel—leaving the movies, hiding away in her apartment in New York?"

"Yes, but Garbo isn't a tragic figure."

"What do you mean, tragic?"

"Who knows, Mother. Maybe she is. I don't know anything about Garbo's New York life. That's why she became a recluse, so people would leave her alone. The point is, I mean actresses like Harlow and Duse. Marilyn loves Eleonora Duse."

"Harlow and Duse are dead."

"Mother, let's talk about something else."

It was in 1960 that Marilyn began to come completely apart. Even in the picture Let's Make Love *she looked tired, whereas in* The Prince and the Showgirl *her illness had been completely invisible. By this time the medications Marilyn originally used to help her relax and to sleep had turned against her and were changing her good-natured personality and affecting her ability to work.*

I often wonder whether analysis helped her or made her worse. Inez Melson felt that so much looking inside yourself wasn't a good idea. Ana also. Someone said to me that people with fragile personalities shouldn't do the kind of method training that Lee Strasberg did because it broke down defenses that a person uses to cope with the world. Granted, Lee was complimentary and gentle with Marilyn rather than his usual cutting self. But the sum of it is, there may be feelings that a person buries that are better left buried. I really don't know. If I had to make a choice, I would say that it was not the introspection but rather the destructiveness of the pills that wrecked her that year. But I also know that the eight years of therapy that she'd had at the point she died hadn't created a strong, healthy, self-confident person. In fact, to me, Marilyn had been stronger, healthier, and more self-confident before she went to New York.

Berniece, in a melancholy mood, sifts through the box of dresses that Marilyn has sent. They are not the usual assortment of glamour outfits. Folded neatly on top is the glittering gold lame gown Marilyn wore to receive the *Photoplay* award for "fastest rising star." But underneath are vestiges of the domestic lifestyle Marilyn attempted in recent years: maternity dresses. They are feminine, modest, with small weights sewn in the hems. Marilyn has been sweeping memories out of her closet.

Berniece reviews the hopes and the failures: the tubal pregnancy in Amagansett, Long Island, after *The Prince and the Showgirl* was finished; corrective gynecological surgery in New York so she could try again; a second miscarriage at the end of *Some Like It Hot*; another ordeal with corrective surgery; a ten-day hospitalization in Los Angeles during the filming of *The Misfits*. The divorce from Arthur in January. The recent nervous exhaustion and an unhappy stay at Payne Whitney, then a transfer to Columbia-Presbyterian Hospital for three weeks in February. Finally a change in the atmosphere, as Joe DiMaggio reappears on the scene like a white knight.

101

Marilyn spent three days in Payne Whitney, in a section for psychiatric disorders. The episode was not at all what she had planned. Instead of the several days' rest she wanted, she felt she had been imprisoned. So, with Joe's assistance, she had herself transferred to Columbia Presbyterian to carry out her original plan.

Miraculously, Joe and Marilyn are coming to Florida. Berniece's mood is transformed from melancholy to tenuous delight. Can Marilyn and Berniece outwit reporters in St. Petersburg this spring of 1961? Three times in one day they brainstorm on the telephone to arrange a rendezvous. Finally the plan is set: they will meet in the parking lot outside Marilyn's hotel. "I'll watch from the window for your car," says Marilyn.

"You watch the hotel door for me. I won't be blond. I'll be wearing a black wig and an aqua linen suit."

Then another call from Marilyn. She is sobbing. They can't get together. Though they have the reporters outfoxed, now the fish are; biting, and Joe has decided Marilyn must come fishing with him.

Maybe tomorrow.

Maybe tomorrow self-assertion will win out over the fish, and the reporters, and the men in their lives.

Illustrations and Family Tree

"These Are Our Memories . . ."

Della Hogan (right) and sister Myrtle, around 1890. Della Hogan was Berniece's and Marilyn's grandmother.

Above: Gladys Pearl
Monroe, age 4.

Right: Gladys Monroe,
Berniece's and Mari-
lyn's mother. At age
16, she married Jasper
Baker, fourteen years
her senior.

Top left: Jasper "Jap" Newton Baker, age 49. After he and Gladys divorced in California, he stole their children, Berniece and Jackie, from her custody to raise them in Kentucky.

Top right: Robert Kermit Baker, called "Jackie," age 2. He was Gladys's and Jasper's first child. After a series of accidents and ongoing illness, he died at age 14.

Bottom left: Della, Jackie, and Gladys holding infant Berniece, around 1919.

Bottom right: Gladys, holding Berniece. Her brother Marion Monroe is holding Jackie.

Above: Gladys (right) with a friend on a California beach, 1924.

Left: Postcard from Della mailed from Borneo five days before the birth of Norma Jeane in 1926. "This is the kind of big snakes they have here," she writes. "They are big enough they could swallow you & Jackie and so could the alligators."

Top Right: Norma Jeane was 12 when she was told she had an older sister. This is the first picture she sent to Berniece.

Above: Berniece Baker Miracle, age 18. Berniece was 19 and married to Paris Miracle when her mother wrote to say she had a younger sister. This is the first picture Berniece sent to Norma Jeane.

Right: Norma Jeane, age 14.

Norma Jeane, age 16. She dotted the "i" in "sister" with a heart.

Right: Norma Jeane and James Dougherty.

Below: Ana Lower handled the invitations for Norma Jeane's wedding to James Dougherty, three weeks after Norma Jeane's sixteenth birthday. Ana suggested to Berniece that pillowcases would make a nice gift.

Axel Fogg

Miss Ana Lower

requests the honour of your presence

at the marriage of her niece

Norma Jean Baker

to

Mr. James E. Dougherty

Friday, the nineteenth of June

nineteen hundred and forty-two

at 8:30 o'clock p. m.

at the home of

Mr. and Mrs. Chester Howell

432 South Bentley Avenue

Los Angeles, California

Reception
Immediately after ceremony
432 South Bentley Avenue
Los Angeles, California

Above: Paris Miracle, age 23, and Berniece Miracle, age 22.

Right: Letter from Mrs. James E. Dougherty, February 2, 1944. Norma Jeane was stationed with her husband on Catalina Island with the merchant marine.

Portrait of Norma Jeane, age 17. She brought this picture to Berniece when she visited her in Detroit in 1944.

Opposite page:
Norma Jeane and Berniece, 1944.

Above: Grace Goddard was a friend of Gladys. She became Norma Jeane's guardian when Gladys had to be institutionalized, and she also served as Marilyn's first business manager.

Right: Ana Lower was Grace Goddard's aunt and a Christian Science practitioner. She was Norma Jeane's beloved "Aunt Ana," and she welcomed Norma Jeane, Gladys, Berniece, and Mona Rae into her home. The back of this photo reads "Happy Smiles from Happy Isles, July 1939."

Above: Norma Jeane in
her hat with the heart-
shaped brim, Berniece,
and little Mona Rae in
Detroit.

Right: Niobe Miracle
(Paris's sister),
Berniece, and Norma
Jeane, posing in an
atrium in Canada.

Above: Berniece and
Norma Jeane.

Left: Norma Jeane,
Paris, and Berniece.

Top: Berniece and her mother, Gladys, 1946. When Gladys was released from the institution and came to stay with Norma Jeane (Marilyn by then) and Aunt Ana in Los Angeles, Berniece spent her entire savings to fly herself and Mona Rae to California for a visit.

Bottom: Berniece, Gladys, and Marilyn in Los Angeles in 1946.

Family dinner at a Chinese restaurant. Clockwise from left: Berniece, Mona Rae, Grace Goddard, her sister Enid Knebelkamp, Marilyn, Aunt Ana, and Gladys.

Above: An early portrait of the new Marilyn.

Right: Marilyn's ticket into the dream factory.

· 1946 ·
TWENTIETH CENTURY-FOX FILM CORPORATION
BEVERLY HILLS, CALIFORNIA
TEMPORARY AUTOMOBILE PASS
LICENSE NUMBER 93-R-583
NAME Norma Jean Dougherty 11-1-46
THIS PASS EXPIRES UPON COMPLETION OF PRODUCTION
OF STOCK
OR ON
NO. 21
· 1946 · CASTING DIRECTOR
PLEASE SEE REVERSE SIDE

Above: Berniece and Marilyn on the beach at Santa Monica, 1946. Marilyn is actually the taller sister, but is compensating for the slope of the beach by standing on tiptoe.

Center: Berniece, Gladys, and Marilyn.

Right: Three generations: Berniece, Marilyn holding Mona Rae, and Gladys.

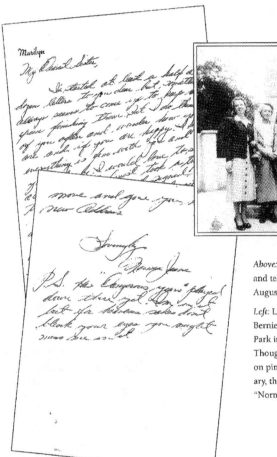

Above: Berniece, Gladys,
and teenaged Mona Rae, St.
Augustine, Florida, 1952.

Left: Letter from Marilyn to
Berniece at Palms Trailer
Park in Orlando, Florida.
Though the letter is written
on pink "Marilyn" station-
ary, the signature is still
"Norma Jeane."

Above: Marilyn gave this publicity still to Paris when he and two men he worked with visited her in New York. Berniece wanted desperately to go, sensing that Marilyn needed her, but policy at that time would not permit wives on business trips. The inscription reads: "For Paris, Love & Kisses from your Sister-in-Law."

Right: Marilyn and Maf. The pup was a gift from Frank Sinatra and named as a joking reference to Frank's rumored connections with the mob.

Right: Joe DiMaggio signed this photo for Berniece when they met in New York in 1961, both keeping Marilyn company after her gallbladder surgery. Joe and Berniece would meet again a year later when they shared responsibility for Marilyn's funeral arrangements.

Below: Christmas greetings to Berniece and Mona Rae from Lee and Paula Strasberg. Marilyn studied the "Method" with them at the Actors Studio, and Paula was her acting coach for several movies.

THE WHITE HOUSE

WASHINGTON

April 11, 1962

Dear Miss Monroe:

Many, many thanks for your
acceptance of the invitation to appear at
the President's Birthday Party in Madison
Square Garden on May 19.

Your appearance will guarantee
a tremendous success for the affair and a
fitting tribute to President Kennedy.

With every good wish,

Sincerely,

Kenneth O'Donnell
Special Assistant to the President

Miss Marilyn Monroe
12-305 Fifth Helena Drive
Los Angeles 49, California

Marilyn sang "Happy Birthday" for President Kennedy.
Shortly after her appearance at the birthday gala, Peter
Levathes at Fox fired her from "Something's Got to Give"
because of her repeated failure to show up on the set.

Rev. Floyd Darling walks
Berniece to the mortuary the
day before Marilyn's funeral
as a photographer scrambles
for another shot.

In Memory of
Marilyn Monroe

Born
June 1st, 1926

Passed Away
August 5th, 1962

Services
Wednesday, August 8th, 1962
Westwood Memorial Park

Officiating
Reverend A. J. Soldan
Village Church of Westwood

Entombment
Westwood Memorial Park

Marilyn's Family Tree

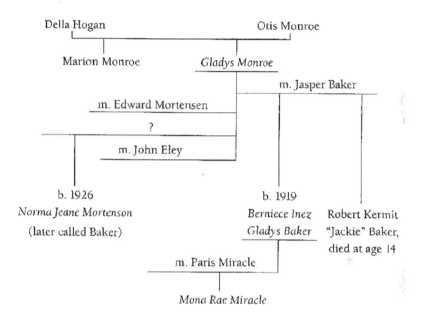

Della Hogan   Otis Monroe

Marion Monroe   *Gladys Monroe*

m. Jasper Baker

m. Edward Mortensen

?

m. John Eley

b. 1926
Norma Jeane Mortenson
(later called Baker)

b. 1919
Berniece Inez
Gladys Baker

Robert Kermit
"Jackie" Baker,
died at age 14

m. Paris Miracle

Mona Rae Miracle

Others

Grace Goddard
Gladys's friend, later caretaker for Norma Jeane, Marilyn's first business manager.

Aunt Ana Lower
Grace Goddard's aunt, a Christian Science practitioner, caretaker to Norma Jeane and to Gladys. Berniece and Mona Rae stayed with her when they visited Marilyn in Los Angeles.

Enid and Sam Knebelkamp
Grace Goddard's sister and brother-in-law, friends to Marilyn. Berniece stayed with them after Marilyn's funeral.

Niobe Miracle
Paris's sister. She was staying with Paris and Berniece and Mona Rae in Detroit when Norma Jeane visited.

Part Four

"I Need You to Be with Me"

Chapter Eighteen

July 1961

A secret visit is in progress. Berniece floats in the world of white that is Marilyn's New York apartment, waiting for Marilyn to appear. She has crept into New York under a fake name to care for Marilyn during convalescence from gallbladder surgery.

Berniece has been giving reporters the slip for more than ten years. Her public appearance now could explode into a maelstrom of public attention and publicity that would agitate Marilyn's condition. The sisters have conspired to schedule their visit for when Marilyn is released from the hospital. Berniece checks into the Park Sheraton Hotel, where she awaits a call from May Reis. When Marilyn arrives home and breathes a careful sigh behind the closed doors of her thirteenth floor apartment, Berniece gets the all-clear signal and immediately takes a taxi to 444 East 57th Street, Apartment 138.

May Reis, Marilyn's secretary, is friendly but businesslike. She welcomes Berniece and leads her through the foyer, across floor tiles of giant black and white squares. In the living room, everything gleams white or, mirrored, reflecting the expanse of white.

"Marilyn will be out in just another minute," smiles May. Her face is bland, matronly, framed by neatly cropped gray hair. "She didn't want to greet you from her sickbed."

Berniece's eyes sweep the room, admiring the ornate carving on the white fireplace, moving up the twin towers of shelves flanking the fireplace. They linger a moment on an enormous oriental painting of a black horse, turn at the white louvered doors between the dining area and the kitchen, and follow the steps of a maid who disappears down a hall with her luggage.

I waited about five minutes. I began to calm down, and I felt a sense of rightness about this, in spite of the difficulties Marilyn and

I had faced in arranging to get together. Marilyn was acting against the advice of Joe DiMaggio, who warned her that we'd be mobbed. I was acting against Paris's advice. He was angry and scared, even jealous.

From the onset of Marilyn's popularity, reporters' voracious appetite for news about her extended to people who were close to her. I habitually had to dodge hit-and-run photographers. I was forced to change my unlisted telephone number time after time after time. Invariably reporters found it out. I worked hard to heed Marilyn's warnings. "Don't let them rip open your privacy," she would tell me. "You are so lucky to have a normal life. I'd give anything to have a normal life like yours." She had been very protective. She had been very strenuous in guarding my privacy and the privacy of our mother.

But for several months I had been aware of a transition in Marilyn's attitude. New problems were coming at her from every direction. In our telephone conversations, her usual wistfulness about getting together had changed to strong invitations, and finally she put it in terms of a specific need that I felt compelled to meet. "I need you to be with me," she said. "After I have surgery, I'll need somebody to be with me, especially at night. It'll give us a chance to talk. I need to talk to you, Berniece, and not over the telephone." So I said, "Then I'll come."

"Be sure to use an alias," Marilyn warned me. "Let me know what you decide on and I'll have May arrange everything."

I was hopeful, and as the trip had taken shape, I had grown determined that I could help her regain her equilibrium.

After about five minutes I heard Marilyn's voice. She came walking in, looking as if nothing were wrong or she'd ever been sick. The only sign was that she walked a little slowly and stiffly. She was wearing a white summery dress and high-heeled summer sandals. She wasn't wearing much makeup, but her hair had been done before she left the hospital so that she would look good for the photographers. She looked very natural and lovely. She smelled as sweet as she looked. She was perfectly adorable.

"Berniece, you're here? You're really here!" Marilyn calls out.

Marilyn and Berniece stand hugging each other. They step back to survey each other, and hug once again, then stand, beaming.

"You look just great!" exclaims Berniece. "How do you feel? Should you be out of bed? Oh, honey, I'm so glad to see you!"

"Oh, Berniece, you look so pretty yourself. You don't age at all!" Both May and the maid have discreetly disappeared.

Marilyn and Berniece are patting and squeezing each other's arms, relishing the reality of being together. They embrace again.

"It's so great to have you here in New York, Berniece, I'm almost glad I had surgery" Marilyn says. She clutches the right side of her rib cage and curbs a tiny laugh. She is trying not to pull her stitches.

Remnants of childhood loneliness are swept away by the keen excitement of the reunion. They anticipate long days and leisurely talks. But it is hard to resist beginning everything in a rush.

"You mustn't tire yourself," declares Berniece. "Let's get you back in bed."

"Oh, no! It seems like I just got out of that old hospital bed. Let me stay up a jew minutes! I want to show you your room, and then I'll lie down while you get unpacked, and then we'll have dinner."

"Honey your apartment is beautiful. I love the way everything is white. And is that your piano that was at Ana's? You've painted it white, haven't you?"

"Yes, the old Franklin grand is now white." Marilyn stops at the piano. "Aren't these gorgeous?" Sitting atop is a vase of bright red anthuriums, the gift of a friend. "I brought them home from the hospital. They're my favorite flower."

"They're beautiful," Berniece agrees.

"Is Italian food okay, honey?'" she asks.

"Sure, I love it."

"My maid, Lena, she's Italian. She's a fabulous cook. I'm really looking forward to having a meal at home again." Marilyn takes Berniece's hand, leading her down the hall to the second bedroom. Before nightfall, however, Marilyn changes her mind,

133

moving Berniece from the second bedroom into the den. On the floor is a bust.

"Oh," Berniece says, "Paris told me about this."

"Yes! It's Carl Sandburg—isn't he wonderful? But I can see why your father-in-law's Lincoln kept moving from place to place. What do you think—should you meet him as you come in, or should he be near his poetry?"

Berniece studies the situation and decides, "I think he'd look good anywhere."

"Thank goodness he's not too heavy. I keep carrying him from room to room. I want him everywhere!" Marilyn laughs.

"This den was Arthur's study," Marilyn explains. Books of all sizes sit in a jumble on the shelves that line the walls. "It has a cozy atmosphere. Here's the TV. The hide-a-bed sofa is very comfortable. This will be more homey for you.

"I'm in the process of stripping that second bedroom," Marilyn continues. "I'm going to take those twin beds to Arthur while you're here. They were favorites of his. We'll take them to him in Connecticut."

Marilyn and Berniece settle comfortably into a domestic routine. Marilyn is the first person awake and moving about each morning in spite of her surgery. The day begins when she steps barefoot into the hallway to retrieve the newspaper. She reads the entertainment reviews and scans the other pages for stories that interest her. Newspapers and magazines cover the top of the coffee table and accumulate into high piles in the corners of her bedroom. She means to spend more time with them later.

Every day except Sunday, Marilyn's maid Lena arrives at eight, letting herself in the backdoor with a key. The first chore on the schedule is to hand wash Marilyn's beige lace bras and hang them to dry. Then she spends the majority of her day in the kitchen.

Just after Lena arrives, Berniece hears hammering and shouting as workers remodel the building next door. She dozes lightly for an hour longer. She will dress and meet Marilyn at the tiny wooden table for two in the kitchen, having toast and coffee while Marilyn plays with a small square of broiled steak, hardly taking a bite.

At the rear of the kitchen, a door opens onto the service hallway. On one afternoon, a messenger knocks there, delivering a warm white box. It holds an Italian dinner, the gift of a newly opened restaurant. An aroma of tomato and cheese fills the small room, but Marilyn says to Lena, "Well, you can dispose of this."

Berniece knows that Marilyn's convalescent diet allows Italian food. Why throw this out? Marilyn pats Berniece's shoulder playfully. "It seems like a waste, I know, but I only accept gifts of food to be polite. I can never eat them because they might be poisoned."

"Oh!" Berniece is silent for a moment, then pretends her distress is because of the wasted food. "It smells so good, I'd almost take the chance."

Marilyn's special diet prohibits alcohol and promotes egg whites. Her doctor has prescribed four raw beaten egg whites a day. Marilyn spoons the white froth from a dessert bowl, and Lena bakes more of the magic egg whites into fresh angel food cakes for Marilyn and Berniece.

Berniece begins to notice how many pills Marilyn consumes and wishes that the doctor had prescribed nothing more habit forming than egg whites. Each evening around dinnertime the doctor comes to call. He stops on his way home from his office, and the visits have a social flavor. After each examination, Marilyn personally mixes him a Scotch and soda. He stays only about twenty minutes.

135

The doctor seemed to delight in having Marilyn as his patient. He was friendly and comfortable to be around, and without hesitating I found myself asking him about Marilyn's sleeping pills.

Marilyn, of course, took a lot of pills while she was in the hospital. At home she was taking as many as ever. Maybe more. At home there were no nurses to supervise her.

I asked him when she would finally get off them. He didn't give me a definite answer. I didn't think I sounded bossy or prying. I was just concerned, and just making conversation with Marilyn and the doctor.

But Marilyn turned to me and said, "I need those pills!" It was a sharp, quick remark. "I have to get my rest," she said.

What Marilyn said—that she needed her rest—was true. I knew that she had difficulty sleeping. She used the pills to help, and for years she used blackout shades and a sleep mask. Still, it was easy to see that there was something unusual about her pill taking. After that incident I was frankly worried.

The daily routine peaks for Marilyn when the doctor departs and Joe DiMaggio arrives for dinner.

Marilyn and Joe have been divorced for eight years. Their marriage ended after nine months in 1954; however, Joe exudes a proprietary air. Berniece meets him on Marilyn's second night home from the hospital and finds him unpretentious and easy to talk to, full of common sense and concern for Marilyn.

Joe, retired from playing professional baseball with the New York Yankees since 1951, is charming. When Berniece leaves, he surprises her with an eight-by-ten glossy photograph of himself in baseball uniform. He writes across the bottom: "To Marilyn's lovely sister Berniece—whose pleasant company was appreciated, Best Always, Joe DiMaggio." He thanks her for their evenings of conversation and punctuates his goodbye with an invitation to San Francisco.

Lena prepares a dinner each evening for four: Marilyn, Berniece, Joe, and George Solotaire, a ticket broker in New York. George is Joe's frequent companion and the most relaxed of the four—friendly, jovial, and good at putting everyone at ease. He has been at Joe's side for many years and was one of the few guests present at Joe's wedding to Marilyn.

Occasionally Marilyn has a cocktail ready for George when he arrives; if not, he mixes his own. Marilyn wears a dress or slacks and shoes with medium heels. The group has a casual meal at the dining room table, savoring Marilyn's favorites like veal piccata or fettuccine Leon. They talk continuously, entertaining themselves without benefit of television or radio, and wind up the meal with hot tea.

Joe always had tea. He drank tea then because of his ulcers. Except for George, we were all tea drinkers, at least at that time. I never saw Joe drink coffee, although I have heard that he used to be a coffee hound during his baseball days, so I guess he was a natural for the Mr. Coffee commercials he did later.

The maid clears the table, cleans the kitchen, and leaves for the evening. The four sit in the living room together after dinner. Before Joe leaves, he and Marilyn will talk in her bedroom for a while alone.

Sometimes when Joe and Marilyn were discussing something, George and I would go into the den to watch TV. We would watch a couple of programs and leave Joe and Marilyn alone. Joe acted as if he were still in love with Marilyn.

"I miss Joe, Jr.," Marilyn tells Berniece when they are alone. "I'm extremely fond of him. When Joe and I were married it seemed that Joe, Jr., loved me more than he did Joe. He would come and talk to me more. He brought his troubles to me.

"He was having the usual young teenager problems," she continues. "Mostly I just listened to him. I loved doing things with him, and I gave him spending money from time to time and little things."

"You're still in touch, aren't you?" asks Berniece.

"Yes. He keeps in touch. He calls. Sometimes he writes. A few days ago I got a great letter. He's twenty now. I just listen.

"I miss Jane and Bobby, too—Arthur's children," she reflects, "but somehow I guess I'm closer to Joe, Jr. I don't know why. I love all three of them. And Patricia, Norman and Hedda's daughter. She's such a dear. He's written about her in his poetry. I'll see if I can find one of his collections. You can look at it tonight when you get in bed."

Patricia Rosten's education will be provided for in Marilyn's will. Marilyn always enjoys being with children. As a bride of sixteen, she impressed Jim Dougherty with her ability to attend to the needs of his nieces and nephews. Mona Rae was delighted with her, as an adult with whom immediate rapport was possible. Fred and Mary Karger's children adored her. Of the cast of *River*

137

of No Return, child actor Tommy Rettig was her best friend. She often frolics with the children of makeup man Whitey Snyder and his wife, costumer Marge Plecher. When she goes to Los Angeles at the end of this year, December will find her still shopping for Christmas gifts for Jane and Bobby.

Chapter Nineteen

Dropping his second tea bag into the kitchen trash can one night, Joe spies a discarded bill and idly fishes it out. He scans over the list of household supplies and wines that have been delivered in the afternoon.

He grumbles loudly, "This bill is not right! It's added up nearly double! Doesn't someone check these things when they are delivered?"

"I don't think that's any of your business," Marilyn hisses, taking the bill from Joe.

She is irritated at his poking in the trash can but admits the next day to Berniece, "You know, it's true. I didn't check that bill when the delivery arrived."

"Well," Berniece falters uncomfortably, "you can't be here every time something arrives."

"I wonder how many times I've been cheated like that."

"Do you check your books or discuss them with your secretary?" asks Berniece.

Marilyn shakes her head slowly. "I haven't been bothering."

Berniece soon discovers Marilyn at the desk in May's office, the apartment's third bedroom, poring over a ledger. She is examining entries thoroughly. Marilyn frowns and shakes her head.

"I seem to be paying for things I don't remember getting. Just like Joe said. I have so many problems. So many problems."

I wish I could have helped her more. That was my field—bookkeeping and accounting. Not that I was any better than May. May was a good bookkeeper. The problem was Marilyn's lack of planning or lack of proper control of income and expenses.

But money was only one of many things that she had on her mind. Every day she mentioned problems, problems, problems. But it was dawning on me that they weren't just chores, things that she expected

*to accomplish and get off her mind, but things that seemed to weigh
her down. I kept listening, trying to figure out what she wanted to
say, and trying to figure out how I could help. I kept waiting for her
to get around to exactly what was troubling her.*

Berniece knows from experience with surgery how a
convalescent feels—bored, sweaty, irritable, worried, subject
to bouts of pain. She soothes Marilyn with alcohol rubdowns
from time to time in the afternoon. She admires the surgical
scar, a small neat line at the base of Marilyn's ribs. Marilyn is not
distressed by the scar. A younger Marilyn was anxious that her
appendectomy scar be hidden, but she will pose for photographs
with the new surgical scar in full view.

Marilyn spends most of her day in the master bedroom, the
largest of the mirrored and white rooms of the apartment. She
lounges in a king size bed, propped against a mountain of six
pillows. "This is the bed Joe and I used to have in California,"
Marilyn says, then yawns.

Berniece sits at the bedside sewing a pair of bedroom slippers
for Marilyn. They are to be travel booties, like the ones Berniece
brought and Marilyn remarked upon. She is sewing them from
two white (to match the room) terry facecloths.

140   "I know you think I go barefoot all the time" laughs Marilyn,
"but I'll wear those out this winter."

Indeed Marilyn is barefoot most of the day. When she wears
shoes, she chooses a medium or high heel. "I like heels instead of
flatties because they're more flattering to the leg. See how much
nicer the ankle looks . . . but I really *love* going barefoot!"

Marilyn insists on getting dressed each evening for dinner.
She enjoys pretending she isn't a semi invalid. Berniece watches
Marilyn survey her closet, pondering what to wear. Her closet
is filled with rows of slacks, blouses, and simple formfitting
dresses, many with spaghetti straps. "I don't like frilly clothes,"
she remarks. "Frilly clothes take attention away from you."

When Marilyn comments that her bedclothes seem sweaty,
Berniece and the maid position themselves on each side of the
acre of bed and change the sheets. Berniece helps freshen up the

bedroom and polishes a small chest of drawers veneered with mirrors.

Berniece gets plenty of exercise. She loves to take Marilyn's energetic poodle pup for walks. He is imprisoned in the kitchen or the bathroom at night, but during the day he frolics through the white carpet, invariably squatting and urinating—without warning—five minutes before his scheduled outing. Berniece chases after him with a bottle of seltzer water from the bar, which Marilyn has showed her how to squirt on the spots.

"What kind of dog did you say this is?" Berniece teases.

"Poodle," chuckles Marilyn. "He just *looks* like a piece of the rug. He didn't like getting his hair cut, so I left it full and fluffy. Now I like it that way."

Some people hear the name and think they've heard "Mop," which is a reasonable description of the dog. But the name is actually "Maf." The puppy's dam is owned by Natalie Wood's mother, a breeder of poodles. The current publicity is that Maf was the gift of Pat Newcomb, Marilyn's press secretary, but the pup was given to Marilyn by Frank Sinatra. Maf is short for Mafia—a joking reference to gossip about Frank's questionable associations as well as a joke about the dog's protective ability. That the pup is a gift from Frank is a secret at this point. The greater secret, which Marilyn discusses with Berniece, is that she plans to visit Frank's home for a rest when Berniece returns to Florida. Frank has offered her the run of his place while he's out of town.

To Berniece, this trip seems one of Marilyn's more tangible problems. Marilyn seems filled with apprehension because of Joe's jealousy, yet eager to go. "You mustn't tell anyone," she confides to Berniece. "Especially Joe. I am going, nevertheless, because I need some total privacy."

Marilyn's desire to avoid Joe's jealousy and her desire to hold his precious friendship place her on a tightrope of her own devising. Her feelings toward Joe are ambivalent. "I feel I have to avoid the psychological confinement that marred our relationship when we were married," she states, in a clinical fashion learned from therapy.

141

Secrets will out, however. With great dismay and surprise and an admittedly tardy sense of humor, Berniece will learn that the whole world knows about Marilyn's trip to Frank's house. But her lips are sealed. A promise is a promise.

"I'm so glad you're here, Berniece. I need someone here with me at night," sighs Marilyn.

But in spite of wanting someone near, Marilyn likes her privacy. She doesn't fraternize with her employees. And at night she closes her bedroom door and locks it.

Marilyn had lived by herself a lot, and it was natural for her to lock her door at night. It was a habit. I left mine open, cracked a few inches so I could hear her if she called, since she was not well.

Because Berniece will be available to handle any emergencies, Lena asks her if she can come to work a little later. The idea seems logical to Berniece. "Sure," she smiles. "That'll be okay."

But Marilyn is up early after all. The following morning she discovers Lena missing and is irritated by the change.

"Honey, I want her to come in at the regular time," Marilyn says testily. "She ought to be here. She's getting paid to be here."

142

Marilyn was peeved, but I never heard her speak crossly to either Lena or May. Although she was reserved and formal with them, she was kind and paid them well. That she paid everyone not only well, but too well, was a conclusion I was reaching very rapidly.

She also didn't comparison shop. She just bought. She paid a hundred dollars for a dress that I would have paid ten for. To get her hair done cost her twenty-five to fifty dollars, when the going rate in a good shop in Manhattan was twelve dollars. And whatever anybody did for her, they charged her three times what they should have.

Charities continually begged for donations. If she didn't give, she'd get bad publicity, so she had to give to everybody who asked her. May came into the bedroom late one afternoon and reminded her that she had made donations to five or six places in just that one day.

There was always somebody making her feel that she had to give money. And she gave it. She couldn't say no.

"They think I'm rich," sighs Marilyn ruefully. "Everyone is begging me for money. I made a trip down to Mexico once and they were begging me there and I donated a thousand dollars to a children's organization. Their mouths dropped open, and they said, 'Is that all you can give?' It made me feel terrible. So I gave them a check for ten thousand."

Is such a gift an offering to the ghost of past loneliness in her own childhood? Marilyn and Berniece have considered this. Of all Marilyn's problems, these are the ones they share: their mentally ill mother, their abandonment in childhood, and now Gladys's vehement letters of complaint.

Gladys has been confined for eight years in Rockhaven, a beautiful and modern sanitarium in Verdugo City, California. But Rockhaven is not run by members of Gladys's faith, Christian Science, and therein lies fuel for perpetual discontent.

Gladys has been officially diagnosed as a paranoid schizophrenic, one who suffers delusions of persecution. The Christian Science precept against the use of medicines feeds Gladys's paranoia; she believes the doctors are trying to poison the patients. Gladys has attempted suicide several times. She has tried to escape. She has gotten into tussles with other patients.

143

Marilyn had assumed the perpetual expense of Mother's care in a private institution since February 1953. Before that Mother had been in the state institution where Grace had placed her in November 1952. Marilyn moved Mother to Rockhaven when her career began to climb and she could afford the expense.

Marilyn and I took pride in the fact that neither of us had ever taken money from the other. She didn't ask it of Paris and me before she became famous, and we didn't ask it of her after she became famous. She paid her own way to Detroit in 1944 for the first visit. I paid my own way to New York in 1961, for what was to be our last visit. Marilyn handled the total expense of Rockhaven, but it would become necessary to take Mother out after Marilyn's death. Paris and I together barely earned more than Mother's monthly bill there.

*It was a wonderful place, but she would have been happy nowhere.
She resented any place where she was confined.*

"I can't finish reading this letter now," cries Marilyn, stuffing
a letter from Gladys back in the envelope and laying it on top of
the stack of her unopened mail. "I just can't finish Mother's letter.
I'll just put it away for a while."

"That's the best thing to do, I'm sure. I used to do that. Now
I usually skim over them and tear them up."

Berniece's thoughts are years away, in the time when her
curiosity about her mother was a sharp ache just below her
heart.

Marilyn continues speaking with eyes closed, frowning. "I
get angry. I know it's irrational. I know with my head that she
didn't mean to turn her back on me. She didn't purposely get
sick. I try and try. The feeling makes my stomach hurt. She . . .
even when she was with me, she wasn't there. When she got out,
I was already grown up."

"I remember how optimistic I felt in L.A."

"We were all so ecstatic that she was out, but she wouldn't let
us get close to her. And I kept trying . . . we did things together . . .
it was so impossible. And I know how difficult it was when she
was with you in Gainesville before she went in again last time.
God, poor Mother . . ."

Chapter Twenty

"*P*eople on the streets shout at me," Marilyn tells Berniece. A shiver follows her words. "I step from a car anywhere in town and suddenly hear someone screaming at me, 'How does it feel to be a murderer!'"

A number of moviegoers fuel Marilyn's frustrations, trying to make her responsible for the death of Clark Gable.

"Last winter it was just about unbearable. And they still do it, some of them. They resent me terribly for Clark's death."

Marilyn had made The Misfits *with Clark Gable the previous year as the end of her marriage to Arthur Miller dragged out. Difficulties plagued the movie set, but disagreements between Marilyn and Gable were not among them. Nevertheless gossip flourished that her tardiness was deliberate and that she angered Gable and strained his frail heart, resulting in his death eleven days after the movie was completed.*

145

"I have so many problems, so many problems," Marilyn drones softly to Berniece. She repeats this refrain each day.

Berniece would love to help, if only by offering Marilyn a sympathetic listener. By now, Berniece senses that the mass of problems needs to be melted away in tiny quantities. She wonders about the true size of the problems. So far she has seen Marilyn worry about Frank and Joe, donations, being cheated by merchants, and their mother Gladys. And now Marilyn aches from unjustified accusations about Clark Gable's death.

"If I can get out from under Fox . . ."

"Is Fox the biggest problem?" Berniece asks. The subject has changed, and yet not changed; Marilyn has apparently followed an association from Gable through *The Misfits* to moviemaking at Fox.

"Yes. I guess so," Marilyn nods. "I want the contract finished. Two more movies to make for them. I feel like I'm crossing out days on a mental calendar. I'll be so glad when I'm out from under that."

Obligations to Fox lead Marilyn to think of work, and when she thinks of work, she worries about her film company, Marilyn Monroe Productions. She has received offers to buy it. She wonders if she should sell. She needs the money, yet she doesn't want to sell the company. She fears making the wrong decision.

"You're too sensitive," chides Berniece gently.

"I know it. That's both good and bad. I try to make it work for me in my acting. But in everyday life, it can wreck me. I've mishandled a lot of things. I regret . . ."

"Well, fine!" Berniece declares. "Regret the things you've mishandled, but don't fret about the things you weren't responsible for. You weren't responsible for Clark Gable's death."

"Oh, honey, I know you're right . . . but . . . well, what do you do when you get depressed?"

"Well, when I have a big problem," answers Berniece, "I pray about it. And then I just do my best. Actually, I've never been too depressed—where I couldn't function. I usually get mad instead."

"It's good to be like that," nods Marilyn. "I think I should be more like that. I don't often feel sure enough of myself to get angry. But sometimes I do."

As Marilyn regains her energy, she feels the need for more activity, and arranges for a visit from her acting coaches, Lee and Paula Strasberg. When they arrive, Berniece perceives still another item in Marilyn's repertoire of problems.

I bounced in from an afternoon of shopping with my arms full of things to show her. And the driver was bringing up my surprise for her. The Strasbergs were there in her bedroom, so I went in and met them and sat down to join the conversation.

Seeing the Strasbergs in person for the first time, Berniece discovers these giants of the theater to be of physically normal size—indeed, on the small side. They look like anyone's middle aged neighbors, yet Berniece is at once captivated by Lee's words—brisk, authoritative—and by the lights and shadows playing on the bonescape of Paula's face.

We chatted about how Marilyn was feeling. Paula asked what I was doing to enjoy myself in New York all alone. We ended up talking for quite a while.

Finally I excused myself, and Marilyn finished the conversation about business with Lee and Paula that I had interrupted.

Her opinion of them seemed to vary. This time she was peeved when they left. And she was disappointed.

The topic of discussion had been some photographs of her that she did not like, especially the type of finish. She said she knew what she wanted and what was best for her. And the prices she had been charged for her photographs were ridiculous.

Money is always jumping its turn as a conversational topic. The miscalculated liquor bill dwindles to insignificance when compared to the total financial picture.

Marilyn sighs a mile-long sigh. "I have no cash." She rambles on, "Once I gave them my AT&T stocks. Lee wanted to go to Japan."

"Japan?" echoes Berniece, wide eyed. "A vacation?"

"To study." Marilyn clears her throat and takes a deep breath. "We're interested in Japanese theater. The techniques. Kabuki. And T'ai Chi Ch'uan. Oriental movement. The controlled channeling of energy.

"Oh, everything is such a mess!" she continues with a groan. "We were going to tape *Rain* this spring and air it in the fall. They scrapped it. They didn't want Lee for a director because he had no TV experience.

"Oh, look at the way things are going," her voice rises in pitch. "*The Misfits* is dragging along in the theaters this summer. People can't decide what they think about it . . .

"Oh, what's in all these packages!" Marilyn makes a sudden U-turn in the conversational mood.

147

Berniece presents a surprise gift to Marilyn, a trim and elegant bathroom scale, white of course. The little bathroom scale brings Marilyn her first real laugh, and she clutches her rib cage to keep her tender scar from stretching.

"Uh oh! You mean I'm overweight! Is that why you're giving me this?"

Marilyn scoots off the bed and steps onto the scale. "Hmm, well, I was before I went into the hospital, but I don't think I am now."

She grins proudly; she has indeed lost a few pounds. Now she can eat her small broiled steak for breakfast and her salad for lunch with enthusiasm.

"Don't I look better?" asks Marilyn. She seems to appear totally recovered. A professional French masseur has just left the apartment, and Marilyn's face is glowing pink from the facial massage. "I feel sooo much better," Marilyn croons.

Marilyn describes how the masseur gives her a special facial massage. She finds massage to be a fine therapy for sagging spirits. In future months, her friend Ralph Roberts will assist her in California with massage and moral support. Ralph is a fellow actor Marilyn has met through Lee and Paula. He weathered *The Misfits* with her. In a few days Berniece will meet Ralph, and she, too, will feel a camaraderie with him that, like Marilyn's, makes him "nearly family."

Marilyn progresses normally in her recovery from gallbladder surgery. On some days, Berniece stays inside the apartment all day with her, but as Marilyn begins to feel stronger, Berniece goes out more frequently to give her sister the opportunity for some private time.

The doorman hands Berniece to a uniformed chauffeur employed by Marilyn. He takes her to the post office, to matinee performances of plays, to the stores on Lexington Avenue and Fifth Avenue. She prefers to go out only during the day.

"Daytime outings are safer, for an unescorted woman, don't you think?" Berniece says to Marilyn.

"Yes, but why not let me get you an evening escort?" offers Marilyn.

148

Berniece declines. "No, I want to be with you at night." She feels that the purpose of her visit is to see that Marilyn won't be alone in the apartment at night.

"But I'm better," insists Marilyn. "In fact," she says, "let's all four of us go out to a night club and restaurant! You and I and Joe and George!"

When she proposes the idea to Joe, he shakes his head determinedly. "You'd be mobbed! Absolutely not."

The handiest indoor diversion is grooming.

"Berniece, let's do something different with your hair."

"What? What are we going to do?" Berniece is game for suggestions. Playing around with makeup and hairstyles is fun, a favorite activity for her and Marilyn. Berniece has let her butter yellow mane grow for the past five years. Usually she pulls it up into a high bun.

"It's too severe, I think," Marilyn decides. "Your silhouette would look more balanced with more mass around your head. I'm going to call Mr. Kenneth for an appointment for you."

Marilyn wanted me to have the works—a manicure, a pedicure, everything—but I didn't feel that extravagant. I certainly made a change though. The driver didn't recognize me when I came out!

149

Berniece has shed her office manager appearance. The new hairdo is a bouffant pixie.

"I love it!" Marilyn exclaims. She goes exploring in Berniece's closet, surveying each of the garments Berniece has brought, looking for something to set off the new hairdo. She hangs out a pert sundress. "Wear this one for dinner tonight, okay?" Stretching out the dress gently for a better look, stroking the fabric, she continues dreamily, "Oh, I wish Joe would let us go out. I wish I could show you off . . ."

Chapter Twenty-One

"*B*erniece, you and Paris have had experience with buying and selling houses." Marilyn leans across her nearly empty plate of lasagna. "I want to know what you think of my getting a house. I've been thinking about it for months."

"You want a house instead of an apartment?"

"I'd love the privacy of a house. It would seem more really mine. I could have fun decorating it. I loved decorating the house in Connecticut."

"A house here in New York?" Berniece's tone rises a note higher, conveying a growing disbelief.

"Maybe," Marilyn says. "Look. Come over here and look down." She pushes away from the table and goes to the open window. "There's a little house with a yard around it."

Berniece smiles at Marilyn's eager face and peers out. The house is so far down that she can just barely make out a microscopic ring of green around it.

"That's what I'd like to have!" Marilyn exclaims. "Right here in Manhattan. You can see I'm not the first one ever to think of it."

"Well, if you had one in California," Berniece voices her thought with diplomacy, "you could have a bigger yard."

"California would cost a lot less," Joe offers, "and it would be a better place to live for making pictures."

"I know I'd have to go back and forth between New York and Hollywood, regardless of where I had a house," sighs Marilyn. "I just want a place I can call home."

"Berniece," Joe says, "do you know how much a house like that would cost in New York?"

"Brick, you mean, a single family home, right here in the middle of Manhattan?"

"It would be astronomical!" Joe booms, waving his arms.

Berniece runs her mental calculator and supplies a specific figure. "Five hundred thousand dollars" she says soberly.

Joe laughs in appreciation. "Good guess. You're only fifty thousand dollars off."

"Where do you think you're going to be doing most of your work in the future?" Berniece turns the matter over logically. "Do you plan to continue studying with the Strasbergs?"

"I just want a place I can call home," Marilyn repeats. Then Marilyn asks, "What do you think of me starring in a movie with Marlon Brando?" Berniece's question to Marilyn about future work has sparked a connection with Brando.

"Marlon Brando doesn't seem to be your type of leading man," Berniece says, then stops herself. "I guess I have a tendency to typecast just like the studios. But it seems to me that you're more the light comedy and musical person, and I really don't see anything wrong with that."

Marilyn laughs merrily at Berniece's discomfort. She shifts to another subject and says, "I had an offer to do my own TV show weekly. Joe said it would give me too much exposure." She laughs again suddenly. "Do you suppose he was making a joke?"

Berniece turns the conversation back to the house—a topic she is more sure of. Future profit concerns Berniece. Practicality concerns Joe. Marilyn is interested in these aspects of home buying, too. She appreciates good business sense. However, her overriding motivation is to have a private place to call her own. Again and again the conversations at dinnertime turn to the topic of the house. Berniece and Joe begin to see this desire as Marilyn's yearning for stability. "When we were decorating the Connecticut house, I didn't think of anything else," explains Marilyn. "Decorating chases all my worries away. I was just completely immersed. It's my dream now to have a real house of my own."

Just talking about the house seems to make Marilyn happy. Berniece encourages her when the conversation turns in that direction. It is a pleasant compromise. In contrast to their talks during the early years of Marilyn's film career, when Marilyn became animated over matters of face and hair and clothing, now she is absorbed by unpleasant business matters. Her mood usually ranges from somberness to downright discouragement.

As Marilyn plans their trip to Roxbury Connecticut, she grows pensive. "Things were never the same after I saw Arthur's note about me."

"You mean the note in the diary?"

"Yes."

Marilyn recalls, hashing it over again, the entry in Arthur's journal she read during the filming of *The Prince and the Showgirl*. Confided first to friends, it will ultimately come to life again in Arthur's play, *After the Fall*. He had written honestly but carelessly of his impatience with Marilyn, and her reaction on reading it had serious consequences for their relationship.

"Yes. The note in the diary. And some other ones that were shocking," she continues. "I was shocked beyond words. I was looking at some papers on the desk, accidentally at first. I just happened to see . . . I saw these horrible things he had written. I just couldn't believe it!"

"What do you mean, 'horrible'?"

"Do you think being called a 'bitch' is horrible?"

"Arthur called you a bitch?"

"Well, he said he agreed with Larry that I could *be* a bitch."

In Marilyn's mind, Olivier was guilty of several offenses. She said he was behaving as if afraid she would take attention away from him. He spoke to her as if she were simpleminded and made light of her questions about her character's motivation. Evidently Arthur felt caught in the middle. When it became apparent that Arthur considered the movie a trivial entertainment and her character without substance, Marilyn felt betrayed because she was trying to do a perfect job.

She knew she'd overreacted to the journal entry. And she was angry at herself for allowing it to continue to eat at her. She knew how she wanted to view the episode and really was trying.

"I mean, my reaction was horror, Berniece. You know, a woman wants her husband to bolster her up, not magnify her flaws. I should have said . . . I wish I could have just said 'Arthur, you go try to act with Larry and I'll sit here and write about how you handle the experience!'"

Berniece nods her head but remains silent. She's wondering if their trip to Roxbury is about to be canceled. Marilyn says, "I really need to stop thinking about this."

Sweeping Arthur from her mind temporarily, Marilyn struggles to talk to Berniece about something else important. Perhaps her feelings of anger and betrayal have led to this topic. A piece of information she has been saving begins to choke her; it seems stuck in her throat like a tiny fish bone.

Marilyn had finally met her father. She brought up the subject of the meeting several times, beginning to talk, and then cut herself off, saying, "Oh, well . . ." Sometimes she just let the thought fade away. Then it was a very tired "well . . ."

"I feel . . . it was a very important event in my life," Marilyn's voice quavers. 'I wouldn't say it was exactly . . . happiness . . . that I felt. As far as my feelings toward him . . . I don't think I can . . . express it. I guess . . . perhaps I'm not sure what the feeling was.

"The first time I saw my father," she continues, her voice gathering energy, and perhaps resentment, "I was lying flat on my back in the hospital. I looked at him and I studied his face and features, and I saw that Mother had told me the truth, that he was my father."

"I said, 'My ears are just like yours.' You know how the tops of my ears are thin. They don't curl over; they just sort of stand up. I keep them covered most of the time."

"We talked . . . a long time," Marilyn speaks haltingly again. "I enjoyed talking . . . with him."

I don't know how he came to be there, what the reason was that he finally revealed himself to her, whether he came on his own initiative, or whether she had asked him to come. She never got that far into the conversation. She kept breaking off.

She gave me the impression that he was friendly but not particularly loving or affectionate toward her. It was a mutually pleasant meeting, and they spent the time talking about the past.

153

"I was pleased," Marilyn sniffs with finality. "Oh, well . . ."

That is as much as she can express. In her hesitations, there is eloquent questioning. The meeting has resolved a lifelong quest, and yet it has not.

Berniece waits, her attention fixed.

"It satisfied my curiosity . . . well . . ." Marilyn cuts herself off once again.

Berniece struggles to form the right comment. "Did he . . ."

"You must promise me, Berniece, not to tell anyone who he is."

"I promise."

"On your word of honor."

The feelings of resentment that Marilyn shoves into the background do not leave her. They fester. They reassemble and assault her again. Now the dam breaks.

"I'm going to change that will they showed me!" shouts Marilyn. "I want to work on a will to get it the way I want it!"

Of all the sources of Marilyn's frustrations, the greatest irritation during this period of recovering health is the matter of her will.

"They tried to rush me into signing a will just before I went into the hospital," Marilyn fumes to Berniece. "They kept insisting."

"For the surgery?"

"No! When I was going to Payne Whitney. My secretary and my attorney stuck a will in my face to sign as I was going out the door. It was already made.

"I was furious! I told them I was not going to sign it! I stood and argued."

Marilyn was not satisfied with the will and always intended to change it. The right circumstances simply didn't present themselves in time before her death. It was easy to allow other problems to have priority over the will. The appointment she made to discuss changes with her California attorney fell on the day after her death.

Marilyn grows enraged in the telling of the incident, becomes aware of her emotional state, grows tired, and breaks off. Berniece is left puzzled. Little does Berniece know that fate is setting her up to be haunted for the rest of her life by Marilyn's intentions for her will.

Chapter Twenty-Two

*F*ree at last! This is Marilyn's first ride in the open air in weeks. Ralph Roberts—friend, masseur, confidante, and presently a sometime actor—will drive Marilyn and Berniece to Roxbury, Connecticut, in a station wagon. Ralph fills a trailer with a load of things for Arthur. Among them are a favorite chair and the twin beds, leaving the guest bedroom empty.

"I'm sorry," Marilyn says. "I'm sorry we're running late. I found some more things Ralph has to load into the trailer. We're running an hour late."

The day before, Marilyn had told me we would leave at 9:00 a.m. It made no difference to me what time we left, but Marilyn got anxious and apologetic. She certainly got no joy out of making anyone wait, contrary to the well worn theories created by some armchair analysts.

156   They head out for Connecticut. They are going to the farmhouse that Marilyn and Arthur had remodeled, the house that Marilyn had signed over to Arthur during their divorce. "I wanted him to have it," Marilyn explains to Berniece. "It seemed right that he should have it. I didn't want anything."

Like a queen on her Egyptian barge, Marilyn reclines in the back of the wagon. Marilyn Cleopatra wears tan slacks and a print blouse knotted at the midriff. On her head is a bandana anchoring a black wig.

When they stop for gas, a filling station attendant stares. "Do you think he recognized me?" whispers Marilyn. Berniece begins to catch some of Marilyn's nervousness. She remembers Joe's warning about the possibility of being mobbed. For a moment her heart creeps up into her throat, but once on the highway again, she relaxes.

Marilyn was in a lighter mood than she had been in a couple days before, and she was chattering away, yet I was aware that she wasn't going into anything deeply personal. Her conversation while Ralph was with us was like her conversation when May or Lena was in the room.

Marilyn told me she never talked to anyone about her personal life. And I never observed her discussing intimate matters with her employees. The truest thing that has been written about her since her death is that she had a wall around her.

She had a wall around her in the sense that she was comfortable playing "Marilyn Monroe, Actress" in public, and that gave the impression that she was open and congenial. In real life, she was shy with strangers and wary of all but a very few people.

Another true thing that has been said is that Marilyn was dull company at parties. She had no interest in small talk, nor did she have any talent for it. She was good at inventing quotable remarks, but not good at producing them under tension at a party.

When her career became fully developed and her fame was at its height, she consciously built the wall higher. She came to see that she could not trust everyone. She kept her intimate business to herself. And this privacy should be the right of any person. Her shyness and reserve could easily be interpreted through a stranger's eye as coldness, but with trusted friends she could show her real enthusiasm and chatter for hours.

157

When they arrive at the Roxbury farm, Marilyn and Berniece stroll up the hill a short distance, while Maf has a romp and Ralph takes photographs. Marilyn tosses the black wig aside. With the white two-story house in the background, Marilyn and Berniece stand smiling with their arms around each other's waists.

The photographs Ralph snapped that day were the last we ever made together. I was never to see them. Ralph soon moved to California. He sent the photographs and negatives to Marilyn in New York. Did he keep copies or negatives? He said not, in his letter to me after Marilyn's death. When Marilyn moved to California, did she take the negatives or leave them in New York? They disappeared into the melange of personal effects that went into storage while Marilyn's will was in probate.

Arthur wears an old sweater with elbow patches as he greets his guests, the familiar pipe between his teeth. He gives a tour of the large house, discussing its features, and pointing out the new additions he and Marilyn had made, such as the dark wood beams cross ing the ceilings. Arthur brews tea, and they chat in a sun room decorated by Marilyn with black and white photographs of Arthur. Here and in the hall are posters, advertisements for Death of a Salesman, framed newspaper reviews, and full length photos of Arthur blown up almost to life size.

Solicitous, Arthur asks Marilyn question after question about her health; he's happy that she is well enough to be up and about, and says he wants her to feel truly well. "How are you sleeping? Better? Are you taking pills?"

Marilyn's responses were honest. Her answers were "yes," but she was smiling continually as if she had rehearsed a very pleasant encounter for all of us and was not going to let anything make it otherwise.

"How is Paris?" inquires Arthur. "Does he still travel a lot? He said he was extremely tired of traveling."

"He isn't traveling now," Berniece answers. "And I'm as happy about that as he is. He's still with Hughes Supply, though."

Arthur smiles, one hand steadying his pipe bowl.

Marilyn discusses Arthur's children, Jane and Bobby, and asks if he has made any more changes in the house. Then Arthur circles back to Marilyn's health and the details of her surgery.

They look out the windows to a small white frame cottage, built since the property became Marilyn and Arthur's; it is Arthur's writing studio.

Flashing by the wall of windows are a white streak and a longer brown streak—Maf and Hugo, the basset hound—frolicking past the cottage and heading over the knoll toward the pond, which is hidden from view.

"I'm afraid Maf is going to end up all wet and dirty for the trip back," says Marilyn. "I'll have to tell Ralph." She disappears for a moment.

"I'm not doing much writing," says Arthur with a yawn, "but a lot of thinking."

Berniece will wonder later if he was even then composing *After the Fall*. Critics will say that the play is unworthy of him. Three years later, when Paula Strasberg and Mona Rae commiserate over this controversial play, Paula is furious with him. He says in an interview that the destructive portrait of Maggie should not be taken as a factual portrait of Marilyn, but this doesn't counterbalance the public's interpretation. "I don't see how he could have written it," Paula will say. "I have to *make* myself believe he did it! I guess he had to, to get something out of his system. I know the artist has to create." Paula tapers off. "But I can't condone it."

But what are the dynamics of the relationship between Marilyn and Arthur on this day in Roxbury? Marilyn still resents the critical remark Arthur wrote in his journal, a resentment she carried through the remaining years of their marriage and continues to harbor. Yet she has generously taken it upon herself to bring a load of belongings to Arthur, unasked. She seems to enjoy showing Arthur off. Berniece wonders if she devised this trip to display the trappings of stability in her life.

Ralph tends to Maf and unloads the furniture during the visit. He skips the tour, having been to the farm on other occasions, and, after all the tugging and hauling, he passes up hot tea for three glasses of ice water.

Now the empty trailer rattles back to New York. Perhaps the Connecticut visit was necessary to rid Marilyn of things that reminded her of Arthur and to close the book at last on the relationship. Marilyn's mood seems lighter on the trip home.

Back in her apartment, Marilyn climbs upon her bed and cuddles against her mountain of pillows. "I'm so pleased. I've wanted you to meet Arthur for so long. Now you've met both Joe and Arthur. So tell me which one of my husbands you like better." Her tone is teasing, but she insists upon an answer.

"I like them both!" exclaims Berniece, laughing.

Marilyn falls into a reverie. "I wish you could have met Jim, too," she murmurs. "Remember how I used to write you telling you all about Jim? Remember how I used to beg you to come to California?"

Berniece smiles and nods. "And Paris wouldn't budge."

"You've been so lucky to have Paris . . . to be still happily married. I really admire you two. Not many couples get along that well." She sighs sleepily. "Yves Montand and Simone are like that. You and Paris remind me of them."

For a moment Berniece recalls the celebrated scene: Marilyn sitting in the car with Yves at the airport when he left after the filming of *Let's Make Love*, sipping champagne while reporters watched. Berniece had wondered with the rest of the world if Marilyn was in love with Yves. Is tonight a time for recalling lost loves? Or for embellishing reality? Or for make-believe?

Marilyn chuckles almost silently and shakes her head. "Of course the press would rather engineer a marriage crackup than write about a stable one. I was very fond of Yves. He was so charming in a European way, and he seemed to be really fond of me, and that flattered me." She pauses in her wandering and sleepy reminiscences to adjust the pillows and slide further to the bottom of the pile.

"I like to daydream about him," Marilyn drawls. "You know, like you used to have fantasies about . . . who . . . Cornel Wilde . . . like everybody does. That's fun. But what's better is remembering him as my friend. And remembering Simone as my friend. Good friends are rare. So rare."

In her memoir, Simone Signoret will write of the press: "They knew nothing about the quiet lives of the four people in Bungalows Nos. 20 and 21. If they had, they would have seen nothing resembling the blond heart-breaker, or the moody dark man, or the bookworm, or the admirable wife standing on her dignity." She describes the gossip and the reportage as "abysmally stupid."

Marilyn and Berniece once again experiment with makeup, painting faces, comparing age lines.

"Berniece, your teeth are really white. They look so good."

"They're all my real teeth too," Berniece jokes.

They have also been trying on each other's clothing and find that they can still wear the same dress size. Berniece has a lavender dress that Marilyn admires. Marilyn has nothing like it in her wardrobe, and now she decides she must find something appropriate in lavender. She telephones Saks Fifth Avenue and orders several lavender dresses delivered. She and Berniece clown about trying them on and pretending to be models.

As Berniece's two week vacation comes to an end, Marilyn chats with her while she packs her bags. Making an impulsive sweep through her closet, Marilyn gives Berniece a pile of dresses. Atop the pile lie two clingy little nylon jersey sheaths still bearing their Saks tags: ninety-nine dollars, size 12. They have never been worn.

Berniece's farewell gift to Marilyn is cologne. "This is terrific," cries Marilyn. "Joe has given me dozens of perfumes, but I've never had a purse spray before. Thank you."

"Oh, I hope it'll be handy," murmurs Berniece a bit absently. She thumbs through her Hallmark date book.

"You'll have a lot to discuss with Paris," Marilyn says. "Be sure to tell him all about the plays. Tell him I love him. Tell him I said he is so lucky to have you."

Berniece scans the entries in her little calendar. Park Sheraton Hotel . . . RCA Building . . . St. Patrick's . . . Empire State Building . . . got hair done at Mr. Kenneth's—$10.75 . . . Sunday—top Rockefeller Center. The last entry is Eastern flight 619.

Their goodbyes are not sad; Berniece doesn't know that this visit is the last time she will ever see Marilyn alive.

Of the group of dresses that Marilyn helps her stuff into her suitcases, Berniece will dare to wear only one of them in public, a beige wool with a wide leopardskin belt. But at home she models all of them privately for Paris. He does a back somersault on the living room floor, showing that the dresses have literally knocked him out.

Chapter Twenty-Three

February, 1962

Marilyn makes her dream of owning a home real when she places a down payment on a hacienda in the Brentwood section of Los Angeles. She will, of course, keep her apartment in New York. Her heart is there, with Joe DiMaggio, with Lee and Paula Strasberg, with Norman and Hedda Rosten and daughter Patricia, with Arthur's children Jane and Bobby, with Arthur's father Isadore Miller, and with other good friends. The stimulation for her artistic growth is in New York. But the source of her livelihood lies chiefly in Hollywood. And how gratifying it is at last to settle into a real house, a place where Maf can romp in the grass, a place where she can invite friends to lounge beside the pool. She looks forward to eventually having friends stay in a renovated guest cottage; for the time being it serves handily as a giant doggie apartment and storage room.

Eunice Murray assists Marilyn in finding and decorating this Spanish Colonial-style house. Her new housekeeper and companion was hired in November, a middle-aged widow with a variety of skills including interior decorating. Eunice Murray is a longtime friend of Marilyn's Los Angeles psychiatrist, Dr. Ralph Greenson (and Dr. Greenson is the brother-in-law of Marilyn's Los Angeles attorney, Milton Rudin, who was recommended to her by Frank Sinatra). Dr. Greenson's own Spanish Colonial, much admired by Marilyn, was bought from Mrs. Murray and her husband in 1948.

Marilyn moved back to an apartment on Doheny Drive in Los Angeles in November with determined house-hunting plans. In January Eunice Murray discovered one at 12305 Fifth Helena Drive, and when Marilyn decided she liked it, they showed it to Joe DiMaggio to get his opinion. He thought it was a good buy and

162

especially suitable for her, with privacy at the end of the street and a high wall around the property.

Eunice cooks, drives, answers the telephone, keeps the house tidy, and often stays the night. However, in spite of their spending a considerable amount of time together, Marilyn maintains the reticence that is characteristic of her relationships with her employees. Eunice, a self-taught student of psychology who has previously served as a companion to people recovering from stressful situations, respects Marilyn's desire for privacy. The two women now set about planning renovations, buying Mexican furniture and artifacts. Eunice's son-in-law Norman Jeffries is hired as an all-purpose helper.

Marilyn, Mrs. Murray, and Pat Newcomb looked for decorations in Mexico. When they flew down, Marilyn often shopped incognito, but she enjoyed one trip that combined shopping and entertainment by the film people of Mexico. On that occasion she met the film writer Jose Bolanos, and they enjoyed going out together. In Hollywood they attended the Golden Globe Awards together. He was a friend, not a romantic interest, "a sweet boy" in Marilyn's words.

Even with remodeling in progress and without much furniture, Marilyn's house gave her a tremendous feeling of pride. She was so excited that she invited everyone to see it in spite of the mess. Joe DiMaggio was pleased to see her happy involvement and admired each change she made. He was on the telephone with her nearly every day and visited whenever he was in California. Norman Rosten and Paula Strasberg visited. Marilyn was close to her press agent Pat Newcomb, and Pat often spent the weekend. Marilyn had her psychiatrist, Dr. Greenson, his wife, and daughter Debbie to dinner, although a casual tray of tidbits was more her norm. Elegant entertaining was never her style, even in an established household. The Lawfords were her closest friends in Los Angeles.

163

Through Frank Sinatra, Marilyn met actor Peter Lawford and his wife Pat, as well as the other intimates of what is called the Hollywood Rat Pack: Sammy Davis, Jr., Shirley MacLaine, and Dean Martin. She shares their interests in the entertainment business, but not their hobby of politics, though Pat Lawford acquaints Marilyn with her brothers, Attorney General Robert Kennedy and President John Kennedy, and Marilyn has enormous admiration for their drive and intellect.

Another friend Marilyn saw frequently was Ralph Roberts who was in Hollywood trying the movie business again. She called him often for massages, which helped her sleep. One biographer has said that during one of Ralph's visits, Marilyn received a telephone call from a nurse telling her that a man on the verge of death wanted to speak to her. According to this writer, Ralph said the dying man claimed to be Marilyn's father and Marilyn rebuffed the overture.

Marilyn did have mixed feelings about her father, including some resentment—which I feel was healthier for her than that hurtful longing she never quite got rid of. But I don't think that such a call actually happened. She would have told me. A possible origin for such a story is that Marilyn might have said that she resented her father so much that if he were to call from his deathbed she wouldn't speak to him.

Two months after she bought the house, in April 1962, Marilyn began filming Something's Got to Give for Fox. She had made considerable progress since my visit the previous summer when she had been so very fragile, both physically from her surgery and mentally from the aftermath of her divorce and Clark Gable's death.

But post-surgical exhaustion and depression take a very long time to get over, as anyone who has had surgery knows. You wonder if you will ever get your normal energy back. Marilyn's pill taking seemed under control, although it was continuing. Her physician was supposedly easing her off medication. She was taking chloral hydrate as a sleeping sedative. So in spite of her progress, she wasn't truly physically fit. When she hired Mrs. Murray in November, she was still weak, and when she began the filming in April, she also had a virus and a sinus infection.

Henry Weinstein, producer for *Something's Got to Give*, is skeptical of Marilyn's frail health; but George Cukor, who had also directed her in *Let's Make Love*, is sympathetic. Marilyn approves the choice of Cukor, and she has personally selected old friend Dean Martin as her costar. Cyd Charisse, Phil Silvers, and Wally Cox are cast in major roles. Paula Strasberg is on hand as her drama coach.

Preliminary organization is also under way for the fourth film for Fox; *What a Way to Go*, with Lee Thompson as the probable director, may follow immediately. Marilyn has high hopes that the films will be completed according to schedule. If so, by spring 1963 she will have achieved her longstanding wish to be a free agent. So she determinedly faces her obligation, beginning work, however, with the agreement that she will be allowed to go home if her temperature goes over 103 degrees. Her temperature fluctuates during the day and runs between 100 and 101 degrees while she works. By mid May she has been on the set for only six days.

"Sounds like you don't ever have the thermometer out of your mouth," says Berniece. "What do you do after you get home?"

"Putter. Play with Maf. Get behind schedule. Hey! You've set tile, haven't you? I could sure use some of your tile-setting talent right about now."

"I'm so glad you're still happy as a home owner," laughs Berniece. "How's the decorating coming along?"

"Slowly but surely. You'll like it. You'll recognize one or two things."

"You're not trying to do too much, I hope. You need to sit down sometimes and . . ."

"Well, I'm sitting down right now. Guess what I'm sitting here looking at. You'll never guess. An invitation from the White House."

"Well, you can handle that. You've shaken the hand of the queen of England, haven't you?"

Marilyn chuckles. "Peter told me they want me to sing. I'm kind of out of shape for singing."

"Just keep smiling, and no one will notice."

Marilyn had been invited by Peter Lawford to sing at President John Kennedy's birthday celebration at Madison Square Garden on the weekend of May 18-19. It was a great strain for her to go to New York for that celebration, but she was determined to do it.

Isadore Miller escorted her. As always, she looked fantastic. She appeared to be in the peak of health, which she wasn't. Her producer Henry Weinstein was furious. Making such an appearance led him to believe that she had been malingering during her absences from shooting the film.

Marilyn flies back to Hollywood, and works six days out of the next ten. At the end of shooting on Friday, June 1, she cuts her birthday cake with thirty-six candles, surrounded by the cast and crew. Her high temperature doesn't allow her to work Monday, Tuesday, and Wednesday. On Thursday, Fox fires her.

Marilyn had been pleased with having her friend Dean Martin as co-star, but she hadn't liked the script; and what she disliked more was the fact that they began shooting while writers were still working on revisions. She was irritated at being cast in yet another stereotyped role, and she considered the film a warmed over version of a previously outdated movie. She was bound by a contract negotiated six years before, insulted that Elizabeth Taylor was getting a salary for Cleopatra ten times as large as her own salary of one hundred thousand dollars. In spite of all these dissatisfaction, Marilyn had been cooperating the best she could. But Weinstein unfortunately decided to interpret her absences as defiance.

Marilyn got her attorneys busy trying to resolve the situation. While they negotiated, she flew to New York. She discussed the firing with Lee and Paula. She visited classes. She found the courage to decide to audition for the Actors Studio in September.

Surprisingly, Marilyn's dismissal from Fox is resolved rather quickly because Fox's board of directors disagrees with Weinstein and the new head, Peter Levathes. Also, Dean Martin refuses to be in the film without Marilyn. In mid-July they decide to resume production. But shooting can't resume immediately because Martin is off on a nightclub tour that will continue until September.

The days following Marilyn's reconciliation with Fox executives are busy ones. She reads possible properties that are sent to her and considers nightclub offers. She has frequent appointments with Dr. Greenson and her physician Dr. Engelberg for an ongoing virus. She fills many hours with telephone calls to friends in New York; one special routine is to call Isadore Miller each Sunday. In addition to shopping and continuing the decorating projects, Marilyn has interviews and cover photography sessions with a number of magazines, among them *Vogue, Cosmopolitan,* and *Life.* She works with photographer Larry Schiller to promote her impromptu nude swimming photos taken on the set of *Something's Got to Give.* During the *Life* interview in July, Marilyn consigns image making to the background with the perceptive writer Richard Meryman. She sets aside the glamor image and dumb blond gaiety and speaks with him in a straightforward, analytical manner. She rates his August 3 article the most accurate and gratifying profile ever done on her.

Marilyn's trademark gaiety and energy seem missing from these days, but she is fully occupied and seems to be coping well, looking forward to the future. The events of the two days before August 5 give no hint of her coming death.

On Friday, August 3, Marilyn telephones attorney Milton Rudin and sets an appointment for the following Monday to make revisions in her will. She telephones her designer's salon to schedule a session at her house, also on Monday, to work on a dress. Around noon on Friday, Jule Styne calls from New York. The composer of *Funny Girl* wants to discuss the possibility of her appearing in a musical version of *A Tree Grows in Brooklyn* with Frank Sinatra as co-star. Marilyn tells Styne that she will be in New York on Thursday, staying with the Strasbergs; she and Styne plan a meeting for 2:30 Thursday, August 9. She chats with Norman Rosten, saying she hopes to see him and Hedda while she is in New York. She goes out to a session with psychiatrist Dr. Greenson in his office. She visits Arthur Jacobs' office to view a film directed by Lee Thompson and decides to meet Thompson. Arthur Jacobs agrees to set up a meeting for 5:00 p.m. on Saturday; later he telephones her and changes the meeting to 5:00 p.m. on Monday. She telephones Peter Lawford and makes plans to go to a Washington, D.C., theater with him and Pat for the premiere of *Mr. President* on September 27.

Friday evening Pat Newcomb arrives at Marilyn's house to spend the night. Dr. Engelberg stops in, gives Marilyn an injection to help her sleep and, because the chloral hydrate has apparently not been working, writes her a prescription for twenty five Nembutal capsules.

Eunice plans to stay over Saturday night at Marilyn's, as is her occasional custom, and arrives the next morning with her overnight articles. Pat has slept late nursing a case of bronchitis and lounges by the pool during the afternoon. In contrast to Pat, Marilyn has not slept well, and takes pills to calm her nerves. Marilyn putters around the house all day, plays ball with Maf, and is pulling weeds when Larry Schiller drops by. Dr. Greenson pays a call at about 5:00 p.m. and spends an hour talking in the bedroom with Marilyn. At about 7:00 p.m., Marilyn receives a call from Joe DiMaggio, Jr., who is in great need of a sympathetic ear. He has broken his engagement. Marilyn tells Eunice she is happy with the news (Joe, Jr., is too young to be getting married, Marilyn feels) then telephones Dr. Greenson to share the news with him also. Joe DiMaggio, Sr., has just moved back to California, having quit his job on August 1. Joe's former employer, Valmore Monette, will tell DiMaggio's biographer that Joe told him he quit to return to California and marry Marilyn again.

Marilyn, declining supper as she had declined lunch, takes one of her telephones with her into her bedroom. Between 9:30 and 10:00 p.m., Eunice answers the telephone in the guest bedroom opening onto her own, and speaks to Milton Rudin, telling him that Marilyn is at home but is resting in her bedroom. Rudin agrees that Marilyn should be left undisturbed.

Sleep is an elusive blessing. To prepare for it, Marilyn's custom is to take her sleep drug, put the two telephones in the guest bedroom, lock her door, then don her sleep mask and sleep bra.

But tonight, at some point, the routine will go awry. Somewhere between late Saturday and early Sunday, Marilyn dies.

By her account, Eunice awakens sometime after midnight and discovers a telephone cord running under Marilyn's locked bedroom door. Alarmed, she telephones Dr. Greenson, who tells her to go outside and try to look through Marilyn's bedroom window. Eunice sees Marilyn lying diagonally across the bed, face down, nude. Dr. Greenson arrives, breaks the window, and unlocks the poolside door to the bedroom. Marilyn's physician is then summoned, and it is he who pronounces her dead. His call reporting Marilyn's death is logged by the police department at 4:25 a.m., Sunday, August 5.

Taking the call at the police department, where Marilyn's first husband Jim Dougherty has been a respected member of the force since his discharge from the merchant marine, is Sergeant Jim Clemmons, a friend of Dougherty's. Clemmons immediately drives to Marilyn's house to verify the misfortune and then back at the station telephones his friend. On this night Jim turns to his second wife Pat, with whom the subject of Marilyn has not been discussed for sixteen years, and breaks the taboo: "Say a prayer for Norma Jeane. She's dead."

The bottle of Nembutal capsules, obtained on Friday, sits empty beside other pill bottles on Marilyn's bedside table. The autopsy will show a lethal level of barbiturates in Marilyn's bloodstream and in her liver, but no residue in her stomach. The cause of death will be entered as "Probable Suicide." In the past Marilyn has accidentally overdosed and suffered respiratory failure, and the prior two years of crises and depressions offer possible motives for suicide. But the absence of a note, the lack of proper dress and makeup, and a full schedule of appointments for Monday, all seem to indicate an accident.

The stretched-straight-out position of her body, uncharacteristic of a drug overdose, suggests a third possibility to veteran officer Clemmons; he thinks that at the least, someone may have tampered with the death scene. With Clemmons' suspicions, the cloud of chaos begins to mushroom. It will unfold its morbid blossom and will disperse its fallout particles of confusion, lost reports, mishandled procedures, controversies, discrepancies, and rumors for untold years to come.

Clemmons leaves Marilyn's house, and assembled there now—in addition to Eunice, Dr. Greenson, and Dr. Engelberg—are Sergeant R. E. Byron and his detectives; Pat Newcomb, Milton Rudin; and Inez Melson, Gladys's conservator. Inez telephones

169

Berniece in Florida. There is no answer. Eunice calls Norman, who has been working on renovations, to board up the broken window, but he cannot complete the repair before a photographer gets a shot of the rumpled bed. Within minutes the grounds are ascramble with press people.

Part Five

"Marilyn Monroe Was a Legend . . ."

Chapter Twenty-Four

Berniece and Paris, each lugging a heavy suitcase, shuffle into their stuffy house, which has been sealed during their week's vacation. They've heard the telephone's insistent ringing since they pulled up in the driveway. When they open the door, the ringing seems to double its intensity.

It was Niobe calling from Lousiville, Kentucky, to tell me Marilyn was dead. She said, "The news is full of it. She died with her hand on the telephone, honey. I know she must have been trying to call you."

I gave the phone to Paris and went to turn on the radio. I heard the news of Marilyn's death immediately, and I stood there listening to the account of the overdose of sleeping pills while Paris was hearing it from Niobe on the telephone. As soon as we hung up with Niobe, the phone rang again, and this time it was Mona Rae.

I held back from collapsing. I was numb. I couldn't believe that the L.A. officials hadn't let me know of Marilyn's death before they released it to the press. But they had tried to reach me and I wasn't home when they called. The whole world knew about it before I did. We had been traveling for two days in a car with a broken radio.

The telephone rings continually, along with the doorbell. Paris at Berniece's side and Mona Rae, pacing the floor five hundred miles away, are both riding a roller coaster of emotions: fear, grief, a desire to comfort Berniece. To leave her own phone line open, Berniece goes to a neighbor's house and calls Mona Rae. She tells her to stand by to be ready to fly to Los Angeles with her.

Friends arrive, offering to help, attempting solace. Paris stations himself on the front portico, sorting out friends from reporters. Berniece's minister offers to fly with her to Los Angeles. Paris makes telephone calls to Jacksonville and Tampa airports, because the one in Gainesville is shut down due to an Eastern Air Lines strike.

We called the L.A. sheriff's office. In response we got a telegram from the county coroner. He asked if I would release the body to Joe DiMaggio, since it would be hours before I could get there. I wired back, saying of course I would. I got a telegram from Joe. He asked if he could help with arrangements and I accepted, and told him I'd be there as soon as humanly possible. I didn't even know where I would get the money for the trip—we had just walked in from a week's vacation. It was Sunday and the banks were closed.

Someone called my boss at the University of Florida and told him I wouldn't be in on Monday. As soon as I got my flight arrangements made, I sent another telegram to Joe. I couldn't make the midnight plane, but I would be on the next one after it. And I decided then, with the little fragment of sanity I had left, to protect my family as much as possible from sensational exposure. So I went alone.

From the door of the plane, Berniece sees photographers running across the tarmac to the passengers stepping onto the runway. Do the reporters have ESP? Or radar? Who told them she is arriving? She looks beyond them, pretending to be oblivious. "Are you Marilyn Monroe's sister?" a dozen voices cry out. Berniece walks briskly past, and they haul their cameras to the next passenger beyond, and the next, and the next, continuing their question. "Are you Marilyn Monroe's sister?"

Berniece can't find Inez Melson, who is supposed to meet her.

Inez had become Marilyn's business manager after Grace died. But then Marilyn's fame grew and her financial affairs became complex, so Inez had said, "You're too big for me now. You should get your own accountant." Inez told me, "I wish I'd kept her. I see now I could have done as well or better than some of them have done." Inez was also handling miscellaneous chores for Joe during the days of funeral preparation.

When I couldn't find her, I wasn't about to stand out in the open with reporters swarming around, so I ducked into the ladies' room.

I stayed in therefore about ten minutes, until I heard the P.A. system calling for me.

Inez is plump, about fifty-five with a short graying brown bob and a somber expression. She escorts Berniece to her car. Inez rummages through her car interminably, shuffling and shifting umbrellas, sweaters, manila file folders, poking through a briefcase in the backseat. Inez says she has forgotten something and must go back into the airport terminal to speak to her husband Pat who has come in a separate car. Reporters and photographers discover Berniece left standing alone on the sidewalk and set upon her. There is no escape. In any direction she turns, Berniece's curly blond hair, dark glasses, and little pillbox hat are met by a battery of ravenous lenses. Inez reappears and stands by while reporters take several photographs. The mysteriously quiet television cameras are riveted upon Berniece.

After leaving the airport, Berniece and Inez drive directly to Westwood Memorial Park where Grace and Ana are also buried. There they see another horde of reporters and photographers milling about. Managing Director Guy Hockett greets Berniece and Inez and escorts them into a closed reception room. Assembled there are Milton Rudin, Marilyn's Los Angeles attorney; Aaron Frosch, her New York attorney; and Joe DiMaggio.

Joe embraces Berniece and says to her, "I didn't realize you could be here so soon."

"I'm glad you came," Berniece whispers, hugging Joe back hard. "We need you."

"I wouldn't have come over and started to handle some of these things if I had known you could get here this soon," says Joe.

"When did you see her last?" Berniece asks.

"Two months ago. But we've talked on the phone. We talk . . ." He catches himself in the present tense.

"How did she seem then?"

"She seemed all right," Joe says. "I didn't detect anything unusual. When I spoke to her on the phone just a couple of days ago she sounded fine. Saturday, Joe, Jr., called her. I was planning to see her on Monday."

Mr. Hockett interrupts. "Before we get started let me just mention, Mrs. Miracle, as next of kin you can give me permission to go to Miss Monroe's home to get any valuables—jewelry, letters, personal belongings, whatever—to keep in a safe until things are settled. It's the law."

"I don't think we'll need to do that . . . I guess . . . Mrs. Melson and I will be going out to the house a little later . . . I'll let you know."

The attorneys assemble the group to discuss finances. The fact is that there is very little cash available, and Marilyn is deeply in debt. Marilyn's bank account balance is about four thousand dollars. There will be enough to cover funeral expenses, but the situation sounds very bleak. There is not even enough cash available to continue paying Gladys's expenses at Rockhaven.

I relied on Joe for comfort. I was so thankful to have him there to help me cope with the situation, even though we were both under great emotional stress. There were urgent decisions to be made within a few hours. And the first priority at the moment was to keep expenses down. Joe went with me into a room of caskets to pick one out for Marilyn. I chose a medium-priced one, about $3,500. It was bronze, very nice looking. We were both pleased with it. From there we went to talk to Mr. Hockett about arrangements.

176

I didn't identify the body. Joe had already done that.

Next Inez Melson drives Berniece to Marilyn's home on Fifth Helena Drive. Eunice greets them and relates briefly the details of the night of Marilyn's death. She tells of seeing the telephone cord running under the locked door, Marilyn's nude body face down on the sheet and clutching a telephone, the nightstand littered with bottles of pills. It never occurs to Berniece to discuss with the police Marilyn's manner of death or the autopsy or to ask to see the coroner's report. She and Inez are here to choose something for Marilyn to wear in her coffin.

There are two closets to search through, one in Marilyn's bedroom and another in the guest bedroom.

Berniece's instinct tells her that color, rather than white, will create the mood that Marilyn would have wished. She chooses an apple green sheath dress of nylon jersey. Berniece and Inez confer about Marilyn's weight loss and the possible difficulties that may result from a clingy soft dress on a body in repose. They don't know what might be available at the funeral home, so they rummage about, gathering much more than they need—half a dozen safety pins, a sheet, and several garments of various sizes and thicknesses—to be used in making the dress conform to Marilyn's normal body shape.

The last item is a wig. Mr. Hockett has told Berniece that Marilyn's hair is so thin and in such poor condition following her autopsy that a wig will be necessary to make her look presentable.

They find all the necessary items. The final look depends on the talented hands and loving care of Marilyn's makeup man and longtime friend Whitey Snyder and her hairdresser Agnes Flanagan.

By the time the little bundle has been deposited at the funeral home, it is nightfall. Inez has made a reservation for two at a hotel.

"I'm surprised your husband hasn't come with you," she tells Berniece.

"We just couldn't afford it. That's the main reason," replies Berniece.

"Well, since there's only one of you, come and stay at my house," she offers. "We'll cancel the hotel." Berniece accepts.

The car winds up the mountains in the darkness, up and around, up and around. Finally the car turns into a driveway. Berniece relaxes gratefully into a patio chair across from Inez's husband Patrick. They chat quietly while Inez prepares the bedroom facing the patio.

The telephone rings. Through the window come snatches of dialogue. Berniece hears Maf's name.

"I'm glad you don't mind keeping him a while longer," says Inez. "I'll call you about him in a few days."

Berniece chats with Inez's husband for a while. She wonders why Inez has stayed so long inside and turns in mild curiosity to the bedroom window. Inez is at the window nearest Berniece, pressing buttons on a small tape recorder.

When I saw that, I went right inside. Inez hastily turned her back and walked out with the tape recorder. I was so absolutely bewildered by all the events of the last twenty-four hours that I was too disoriented to ask her what she was doing. I was terribly upset and fearful, but I didn't leave. I had all I could bear at the moment without getting into a confrontation with the person who seemed to be my only source of guidance under the circumstances. So I stayed.

During the night Berniece lies in bed staring at the ceiling. She hears noises on top of the house. It sounds as though the roof is caving in. She is frightened and stumbles down a hallway to find Inez and tell her that something horrible is going on.

"That's only the raccoons," Inez laughs. "They come down at night and play."

In the morning, Inez says, "I'm sorry you didn't sleep well. I should have given you an aspirin or something. Do you want . . ."

Berniece is by now feeling too apprehensive to allow herself even an aspirin. "I don't want any pills. I want to be aware of everything that's going on," she tells Inez. "I have to be alert to handle difficult situations."

The first stop for Berniece and Inez today is Parisian Florists on Sunset Boulevard. Berniece buys a blanket of flowers to cover the casket, the traditional family tribute. Inez purchases a cross of flowers for a remembrance from her and Pat, then places Joe DiMaggio's order for him, roses for the crypt vase twice each week.

The next stop is the funeral home. Berniece is again engulfed by swarming fans and news people. Then there is the guest list to struggle through and many telephone calls to make.

Inez hands Berniece a tentative agenda for the service. Lee Strasberg will deliver the eulogy, and the complete memorial service will be taped. "Yes," Berniece agrees, "that will be very nice."

"Check over this list," asks Inez, "and see if there are any more names you want to add to it. We followed your instructions to keep it very small and private."

In a moment, Berniece asks, "Who is Florence Thomas?"

"A very nice and loyal black lady who has done some work for Marilyn. I invited her."

Berniece is nodding her head, "Yes, I want to add Doc Goddard and his wife. And Sam and Enid Knebelkamp. Enid is Grace Goddard's sister." Berniece scribbles the names on the yellow legal pad as she speaks, and Inez disappears in search of a telephone.

The guest list is released to the press:

Those invited to attend:

Lee and Paula Strasberg	Pat Melson
Sidney Guilaroff	Berniece Miracle
Al Snyder	Agnes Flanagan
Anne Karger	Florence Thomas
Mary Karger	Enid and Sam Knebelkamp
Joe DiMaggio	Aaron Frosch
Joe DiMaggio, Jr.	Milton Rudin
George Solotaire	May Reis
Pat Newcomb	Ralph Roberts
Eunice Murray	Dr. Ralph Greenson and family
Rudy Kautzky	Erwin and Anne Goddard
Inez Melson	

We sincerely hope that the many friends of Marilyn will understand that we are deeply appreciative of their desire to pay last respects to Marilyn whom we all loved. We hope that each person will understand that last rites must of great necessity be as private as possible so that she can go to her final resting place in the quiet she always sought. We could not in conscience ask one personality to attend without perhaps offending many, many others and for this reason alone, we have kept the number of persons to a minimum. Please—all of you—remember the gay, sweet Marilyn and say a prayer of farewell within the confines of your home or your church.

Berniece Miracle

Inez Melson

Joe DiMaggio

We called Marilyn's housekeeper-companion, Mrs. Murray, to tell her that she was invited to the services. When she found out that we were not inviting the Lawfords, she was very unhappy.

"Well, they were her very dear good friends!" Mrs. Murray exclaimed. "They were among Marilyn's best friends and they should be invited!"

And compared to the disappointment building up in the crowd outside, Mrs. Murray's reaction was mild. I was already regretting saying no to my minister's offer to come to LA. with me, and I didn't have Paris or Mona Rae either. I needed someone to lean on. More than that, I felt I had to have some sort of spiritual assistance. I scanned the phone book and called a small church outside of town. The minister said, yes, he would be glad to come, both to help me that afternoon and at the services the next day.

Rev. Floyd Darling, of the First Southern Baptist church in Santa Monica, arrives in a white Volkswagen bug. He shakes Berniece's hand. Berniece studies his sympathetic face. Berniece confides her dread of having her conversations recorded.

"I could avoid that by staying by myself, but under the circumstances, I'm hesitant about staying alone. I don't know anybody, and I don't know my way around. I don't know where anything is . . ."

Rev. Darling offers to help. She takes his arm as they walk across the lawn of Westwood Memorial Park. The mob of people seems more upset than when they were milling about yesterday. Voices are louder, harsher, angrier, since the guest list has been announced and copies of the plans for the services have been distributed to the press.

"Why aren't you going to let her friends from the industry come?" screams one of the reporters. "The chapel will hold lots more than that!"

"Aren't you going to invite the Kennedys?" another voice booms across the tops of several heads.

"There are people that really loved her out here!" comes another roaring voice. "They want to be there!"

Berniece clings tightly to Rev. Darling's arm and turns her dark glasses to the nearest face. "Well, it's private," she says softly. "And that's the way it's going to be."

Rev. Darling turns his little white car toward the beach, to Santa Monica. He stops at the Miramar Hotel, which he recommends as moderately nice and moderately priced. They go inside together. Berniece reserves a room and pays for it, then they head back to the mortuary.

As we were driving along, he pulled over to the curb and, with all the traffic going by on the street, we just sat still for a few minutes and he said a prayer. It helped me get through it all.

I told Inez that I appreciated everything she was doing for me—handling Mother's affairs, driving me from place to place, making me welcome in her home—but that I had decided to go to a hotel. I explained that the harassment from these crowds had made it simply imperative for my well-being to have some time totally alone.

Because Inez and I had more business matters to handle in the next several days, I gave her a number where she could contact me. I suppose I still nourished an impossible dream of having some privacy, and I was dismayed when she told everyone at the funeral home the next day where I was staying. I was extremely naive. It took me several days to realize that she had the job of giving information to the press agents employed by Marilyn.

181

Chapter Twenty-Five

*I*n the morning Berniece encounters Joe DiMaggio in the hotel lobby. Joe has also stayed the night at the Miramar Hotel. Both Berniece and Joe are too distraught to engage in small talk, but Joe is cordial and kind, introducing Berniece to Joe, Jr., the courteous young man in uniform standing quietly at his father's side. The young man takes Berniece's hand and she looks up into a face whose features are a near mirror of Joe's grieved expression. The mortuary chauffeur calls for Berniece in a black limousine. She feels groggy and is glad to have the icy blast from the car's air conditioner on her face for the ride back to Westwood. With a black gloved hand, she tucks a wisp of blond hair beneath the rim of her cloche hat. She breathes a sigh of resignation as she looks at the giant white tote bag on the seat beside her, the only bag big enough for all she has to keep track of.

Twentieth Century-Fox, the city police force, and a private security agency have all supplied manpower to form a cordon of guards around Westwood. The fans surge against a human wall that circles the mortuary grounds. Rev. Darling meets Berniece as she steps out of the limousine and will stay by her side throughout the services.

Marilyn's body rests easily in the misty blue satin cradling her. Her figure is outlined lightly and trimly in its apple green dress with simple boat neckline and long sleeves—green, appropriately the symbol of life, for Marilyn's face looks rosy and healthy except for the sealed, peaceful eyelids.

Berniece leans over the bronze casket. "I love you," she whispers. "You look so lovely and so sweet."

Three thousand miles away, Marilyn's brother-in-law Paris and her niece Mona Rae read news articles based upon the press release prepared by Westwood:

SERVICES FOR MARILYN MONROE
Wednesday, August 8 1962, 1 PM
Westwood Memorial Park
1215 South Glendon Avenue
Los Angeles, California

Services to be performed by The Reverend A. J. Soldan
of the Village Church of Westwood, a non-denominational
church. Rev. Soldan, who is also the official pastor for the
California Peace Officers' Association, will conduct a private
ceremony limited to members of Miss Monroe's immediate
family.

Rev. Soldan's remarks will be based upon the quotation
"How fearfully and wonderfully she was made by the
Creator." He will also deliver the 23rd Psalm at the request
of Miss Monroe's survivors.

Eulogy by Mr. Lee Strasberg

Berniece sits silently through the service, adjusting her dark
glasses from time to time. Her breathing becomes more ragged as
Lee Strasberg begins his beautifully wrought eulogy.

"Marilyn Monroe was a legend," he begins. He goes on to
say that though the world knows her as "a symbol of the eternal
feminine," he and the small group gathered to mourn her loss
knew her as a loyal friend and colleague, a woman of warmth and
talent and a "startling sensitivity." He describes her "luminous
quality—a combination of wistfulness, radiance, yearning—that
set her apart and made everyone wish to be a part of it."

He closes not with goodbye, for "Marilyn never liked
goodbyes," but with *au revoir*, "for the country to which she has
gone, we must all someday visit."

Silent tears trail down Berniece's cheeks. The dark glasses
are slippery and uncomfortable now. The organ selections from
Tchaikovsky and Gounod, played by Margaret Hockett, are
captured on tape along with Rev. Soldan's benediction and Lee's
words. Berniece trembles from the power of the eulogy.

Rev. Darling takes Berniece's arm as the march begins from the chapel to the crypt site. Behind him and Berniece are Inez and Pat Melson; behind them are Joe and Joe, Jr. In a few moments, the services are over. Guests pass quietly, shaking Berniece's hand or patting her shoulder, whispering comforts.

To Lee, Berniece says, "Thank you so much. I don't know how to tell you . . . thank you for your loving words."

Lee nods, grim faced. Paula squeezes Berniece's fingers. "We'll be in touch. God bless."

"Call me tomorrow if you have a chance," urges Enid, "and let me know when you can come stay with us."

Inez chides Berniece, whispering loudly, "You really hurt Pat and me having that minister walk with you. We could have walked from the chapel to the crypt with you—two hundred feet!"

The following morning begins with a business appointment at attorney Milton Rudin's office. Berniece and Inez step down from the foyer into mounds of carpet, and sink into pillow soft chairs overhung with tropical potted plants. From her supplies in the giant white tote bag Berniece slides out a notepad and her pen. Trying to keep track of all the players in this nightmare is a formidable challenge.

Thumbing to a fresh page, she glances at a list of press people's names she had begun scribbling and left unfinished. She has a sudden flashback to her dazed first night at Inez's house. Someone had called while she and Pat Melson were talking, someone who was keeping Maf. Inez had told the caller to keep him a few more days. Was that Pat Newcomb? Something is going to have to be done about Maf . . .

Berniece flips the sheet over quickly and concentrates on the faces of the lawyers while she makes notes. Mickey Rudin, a heavyset man, seems curt and impatient. She decides that Aaron Frosch, Marilyn's New York attorney, is the more congenial of the two; in any case, Frosch seems more willing to explain details.

Berniece discovers that she is not attending a reading of Marilyn's will but rather a discussion of problems relating to the will. Berniece has already seen in the Los Angeles newspapers a greater number of details from Marilyn's will than are being discussed at this meeting. She learns that she is to receive a bequest of ten thousand dollars, that a trust fund is to be set up for Gladys, and that several other bequests are specified. Before any actions whatever can be taken, Marilyn's assets will have to begin to produce an income. Practically speaking, there is no money to be had.

A nervous tic begins beneath Berniece's eye. She has a mental image of Marilyn rapping her knuckles on the kitchen table and remembers Marilyn's resolve: "I'm going to change that will they showed me! I want to work on a will to get it the way I want it!"

Berniece coughs, stiffens her back, and brings up the question of other wills. None are known to have been made since this one. However, states Frosch, there was indeed a prior will, one made when Marilyn was married to Arthur Miller. The attorneys explain that if the current will is voided, the prior would give Arthur most of everything Marilyn owned.

Aaron Frosch leisurely discusses Marilyn, her condition, his dealings with her, and his trip to Mexico with her to handle her divorce from Arthur Miller. Frosch relates anecdotes to relieve the tension and smoothes back his dark brown hair, chuckling. Berniece smiles wanly. Soon her own attorneys will begin a correspondence with Frosch, a long-distance relationship drawn out for years during the will's probate period. Two weeks hence Berniece will actually see a copy of the will:

185

I, MARILYN MONROE, do make, publish and declare this to be my Last Will and Testament.

FIRST: I hereby revoke all former Wills and Codicils by me made.

SECOND: I direct my Executor, hereinafter named, to pay all of my just debts, funeral expenses and testamentary charges as soon after my death as can conveniently be done.

THIRD: I direct that all succession, estate or inheritance taxes which may be levied against my estate and/or against any legacies and/or devises hereinafter set forth shall be paid out of my residuary estate.

FOURTH: (a) I give and bequeath to BERNIECE MIRACLE, should she survive me, the sum of $10,000.00.

(b) I give and bequeath to MAY REIS, should she survive me, the sum of $10,000.00

(c) I give and bequeath to NORMAN and HEDDA ROSTEN, or to the survivor of them, or if they should both predecease me, then to their daughter, PATRICIA ROSTEN, the sum of $5,000.00, it being my wish that such sum be used for the education of PATRICIA ROSTEN.

(d) I give and bequeath all of my personal effects and clothing to LEE STRASBERG, or if he should predecease me then to my Executor hereinafter named, it being my desire that he distribute these, in his sole discretion, among my friends, colleagues, and those to whom I am devoted.

FIFTH: I give and bequeath to my Trustee hereinafter named, the sum of $100,000.00 in Trust, for the following uses and purposes:

(a) To hold, manage, invest and reinvest the said property and to receive and collect the income therefrom.

(b)To pay the net income therefrom, together with such amounts of principal as shall be necessary to provide $5,000.00 per annum, in equal quarterly installments, for the maintenance and support of my mother, GLADYS BAKER, during her lifetime.

(c) To pay the net income therefrom, together with such amounts of principal as shall be necessary to provide $2,500.00 per annum, in equal quarterly installments, for the maintenance and support of MRS. MICHAEL CHEKHOV, during her lifetime.

(d) Upon the death of the survivor between my mother, GLADYS BAKER, and MRS. MICHAEL CHEKHOV to pay over the principal remaining in the Trust, together with any accumulated income, to DR. MARIANNE KRIS to be used by her for the furtherance of the work of such psychiatric institutions or groups as she shall elect.

SIXTH: All the rest, residue and remainder of my estate, both real and personal, of whatsoever nature and wheresoever situate, of which I shall die seized or possessed or to which I shall be in any way entitled, or over which I shall possess any power of appointment by Will at the time of my death, including any lapsed legacies, I give, devise and bequeath as follows:

(a) To MAY REIS the sum of $40,000.00 or 25% of the total remainder of my estate, whichever shall be the lesser.

(b) To DR. MARIANNE KRIS 25% of the balance thereof, to be used by her as set forth in ARTICLE FIFTH (d) of this my Last Will and Testament.

(c) To LEE STRASBERG the entire remaining balance.

SEVENTH: I nominate, constitute and appoint AARON R. FROSCH Executor of this my Last Will and Testament. In the event that he should die or fail to qualify, or resign or for any other reason be unable to act, I nominate, constitute and appoint L. ARNOLD WEISSBERGER in his place and stead.

EIGHTH: I nominate, constitute and appoint AARON R. FROSCH Trustee under this my Last Will and Testament. In the event he should die or fail to qualify, or resign or for any other reason be unable to act, I nominate, constitute and appoint L. ARNOLD WEISSBERGER in his place and stead.

The date on the will is January 14, 1961. It bears Marilyn's signature and signatures of witnesses Aaron Frosch and Louise White.

The beneficiaries whom Berniece has not met are known to her from conversations with Marilyn. Mrs. Michael Chekhov is the widow of her early acting teacher who had studied with Stanislavsky. Dr. Marianne Kris is her psychiatrist from New York. Poet Norman Rosten and wife Hedda are friends Marilyn met through Arthur Miller. Hedda was with them in England for the making of *The Prince and the Showgirl.*

I wasn't sure why Marilyn had wanted so much to change that will, but when I thought about how upset she'd been about it, I couldn't bring myself to just accept it. I was extremely frustrated, and I confided to Inez that Marilyn hadn't wanted to use that will.

I was in a terrible dilemma. I couldn't afford to contest it. I resigned myself to accepting the will as it stood.

In October 1962, Inez objects to probate, through her attorneys, alleging that the will had been executed under undue influence of Strasberg or Kris, or both. The court decides that no undue influence was exerted, and the will is admitted to probate. Almost twenty years later, on August 17, 1980, the *New York Times* reports that Frosch's handling of the will has been challenged by Dr. Marianne Kris, citing that the estate has dwindled from a onetime figure of $1.6 million to $101,229 in the years since Marilyn's death.

The article was peppered with inaccuracies, but Frosch's statement that most of the money had gone for debts, taxes, and lawyer's fees was true.

Chapter Twenty-Six

"We don't want the press to get hold of Marilyn's personal stuff," stresses Inez.

Berniece and Inez are at Marilyn's home on the day following the funeral, searching through her personal effects, hoping to find notes on a current will.

After the funeral, Inez, who was appointed by Frosch and the court to act as administrator, and I, and Cherie, a secretary who had done some work for Marilyn, spent three days at Marilyn's home checking through all her belongings. I was there just to help in an unofficial capacity.

We sat around the fireplace watching Inez burn papers all day long. Marilyn had tons of papers of all kinds. Some were organized in drawers. Some were just lying around. Some didn't seem important to Inez, and to her it seemed useless to keep them—letters, newspaper articles, scribbled notes on chores to do, and such. Some were important and had legal implications, and Inez sorted those out and kept them.

189

Inez places Marilyn's red leather Gucci shopping bag on the floor beside Berniece. "Put what you want to take home in here," she tells Berniece. "I'll give you some things . . . Here, look through these newspaper clippings and see if you want any of them."

Berniece sits tearfully at her task, hour after hour, as the three women pick through stacks of papers like amateur archaeologists. Berniece's reaction to every scrap that Inez shoves toward her is so emotional that she has small room in her consciousness to take note of what Inez keeps in her own custody. Inez is very businesslike, reading rapidly, sorting, pitching sheaves of paper into the fire, dropping an occasional leaf onto the layers mounting in a pile beside her own chair. She will note later that Marilyn apparently saved every letter Arthur Miller had ever written her.

The sorting job goes on and on, exhausting the women. During the third day, Berniece says to Inez, "Do you mind if I don't come back this afternoon? I'm feeling rather ill."

"Of course not," Inez says soothingly. "You've already done more than your share. Cherie and I are responsible to the courts. You're not. Three straight days have done us in. I'd like to go home myself," sighs Inez, patting Berniece's arm. "There's no reason for you to come back. Just go get some rest."

"Yes. Yes, I need to," agrees Berniece. "But I still have so much to do. I have to see my mother as soon as I can. Look, I'll be back in touch with you in a few days. I'm going to try to take Mother home with me."

"Oh, Berniece, I have to advise against that! You don't know what taking her out would mean." Inez shakes her head, eyes closed, frowning. Inez reminds Berniece that Gladys is comfortable and relatively well adjusted at the Rockhaven Sanitarium.

Berniece pauses a moment, blinking back tears. "I'd just like to have my mother close to me, you know? All my family is gone now except her."

"Well, dear, what are you saying? You still have your husband and your daughter!"

"Oh, yes, of course, of course. And they mean all the world to me. But it's just something different with my mother. We've missed so many years together."

"We'll talk again later like you say. You go and get some rest. Cherie and I will finish up here."

Berniece wishes she could escape. She gets her belongings ready to move from the Miramar Hotel to the home of Sam and Enid Knebelkamp, where she can spend a few days in privacy working on her legal affairs. Her whereabouts have been known for the past three days. She has no telephone in her room and is stalked by a reporter as she ends a conversation with Inez on the lobby pay phone. She must at least find a telephone in a booth where she can close the doors while she talks. She continues to hold the telephone to her ear, pretending to listen, stalling for a break in the reporter's attention, planning her zigzag streak down the street.

In a moment, she strides out the glass doors of the hotel, navigates across two streets of the intersection outside, and darts into a booth near the drugstore. Footsteps clatter on the pavement behind her. She jerks the folding door shut.

"Sam!" Berniece wheezes into the phone. "They're chasing me! There's a photographer at the side door." Berniece tells Sam where she is.

Berniece sees a third photographer watching from across the street. She pretends to dial another number and talk. And another. And another.

In fifteen minutes Sam arrives. Berniece leaps into the car. They drive around a few blocks, then return to the hotel, to gather Berniece's luggage and retreat to the Knebelkamp's home.

With Sam and Enid, at last Berniece can relax. Alone in the small guest room, she gets a full night's sleep after calling Paris and receiving assurance that he is keeping up with his laundry.

Berniece compares Sam and Enid with the younger version of themselves who had sat at the restaurant table to help Marilyn celebrate her freedom sixteen years ago. Marilyn was just twenty then; today she would be thirty-six.

Sam brought in a newspaper and showed it to me. It was a paper from one of the small suburban towns, and it had run a gigantic headline saying, "Joe DiMaggio Buys Blanket for Marilyn's Casket." The blanket is traditionally provided by the family and I had provided it, with Inez standing beside me at the florist's. Had the newspaper lied for newsstand attention? Or was it a mistake? I was so emotionally fragile at that point that I was deeply hurt, seeing the incident as a personal insult.

I was never quite my old self after Marilyn died. For months, tears would start running down my face while I sat in church on Sundays. I would freeze every time the evening news came on television. I just didn't know what they might say.

A good night's sleep in Enid's house is restoring. Enid asks, "When do you want to see your mother? Do you feel like having

Sam drive you up there this afternoon?" Berniece composes herself to visit Gladys.

"It was wise not to get Gladys involved in all this chaos," Sam says. "She seems to be doing fairly well, considering."

Berniece shakes her head with dismay. "I don't know what it is that sets Mother off. There's never any connection that I can see."

At Rockhaven Sanitarium, Gladys spends her days sitting calmly reading, oblivious to the turmoil of one daughter, vaguely aware of the death of the other.

The director leads Gladys into the reception room.

"Hello," Gladys says to Berniece. "I need to go shopping. Can I stay all night with you?"

Sixty-two years-old at this time, Gladys stares unblinkingly at Berniece with alert, bright blue eyes. She is dressed in her favorite outfit, her practical nurse's garb—white dress, white stockings, white shoes—and her head is topped by a neat bun of snow-white hair.

"How are you, Mamita?" whispers Berniece. She hugs Gladys tightly. Gladys dangles one arm about Berniece's waist.

"This is my daughter," says Gladys, turning to the director. She twirls back to Berniece. "When can we leave?"

192 Berniece laughs nervously and looks at Sam. "Well, Mother, can we sit down and talk for a minute?"

Gladys stands restlessly as Sam and Berniece sit down on the flowered couch.

"Enid sends her regards," says Sam, managing a small smile. "And her condolences. We were very sorry to hear about Marilyn."

"Yes," nods Gladys, glaring at Sam. She turns to Berniece again. "I need some hairpins and hairnets. Can we to go Penney's?"

I have never seen Mother shed a tear in all my life. She didn't seem to have the slightest reaction to the fact that Marilyn had just died. It was extremely hard to make conversation with her. Sam and I tried to be as pleasant as possible. We put her in the seat between us because we were afraid she might decide to jump out of the car.

When we went into the store, I went with her everywhere. Even to the restroom.

With that first visit to Mother behind me, I was ready for my discussion of various problems with an attorney. Sam took me to the offices of Dixon, Howell, and Westmoreland, where he had arranged an appointment for me with Mr. Howell. Sam announced that I was meeting a very special person who had a little surprise for me. I was shocked speechless and Sam was delighted when Mr. Howell told me that Norma Jeane and Jim Dougherty had their wedding in his home.

Mr. Howell was very cordial and understanding of my two primary needs. One was advice regarding Marilyn's will and the other was advice on having my mother released into my custody.

Mr. Howell agreed with the other lawyers that it wouldn't be wise to contest the will, confirming that the prior will would be primarily in the interest of Arthur Miller.

"Marilyn is not here any longer to handle Mother's care," I told Mr. Howell, "and she wants out so badly. I want to give her a try outside again."

Mr. Howell suggested that I devote further thought to the matter after seeing Mother a few more times and after discussing it thoroughly with her. Then I should investigate appropriate accommodations for her in Florida, and if everything worked out, steps could be taken to transfer the conservatorship from Inez Melson to me.

Chapter Twenty-Seven

T he fragrance of chicken stew Paris has concocted fills the kitchen. A houseful of family members has arrived to welcome Berniece back home.

After the others have left Gainesville, Mona Rae remains for two weeks, acting as full-time secretary to Berniece, who must immediately reorient herself to her working life at the University of Florida. Mona Rae writes thank you notes to everyone, producing countless numbers of letters.

Mail pours in. However minimally addressed, it continues to arrive, this waterfall of mail that began on August 5. Again and again, to all types of people from all over the world, with all types of motives, Mona Rae sends a message of appreciation. She directs requests for photographs to Twentieth Century-Fox. And to Fox she sends thanks for their special gift of guards at the funeral.

On one evening during this secretarial marathon, Mona Rae takes a break to watch Marilyn on television, a film history composed by Fox. Marilyn's few minutes of footage from *Something's Got to Give* are incorporated into the production. With the exception of these few frames, *Something's Got to Give*, which would have been Marilyn's thirtieth film, is scrapped. Later, with a revised script, it will be shot with Doris Day and James Garner as *Move Over, Darling*.

In another month, Mona Rae will sign her first post-college job contract, in a city where her relationship to Marilyn is unknown. Away from Gainesville she can revel in her anonymity, and she never tells a single one of her new friends. Berniece, however, must remain and endure continued bombardments from curiosity seekers.

Reporters intent on photographs and interviews come to Berniece's and Paris's door. They stalk the house, creep about the lawns of neighbors, park in front for three hours, leave for ten minutes, come back and sit for hours more. Paris and Berniece never open their drapes. They decide they must fence the lot and put locks on the gates.

Berniece will soon reach the saturation point. Her disgust with the monstrous fantasies about Marilyn that spin themselves out of vapor will reach its peak for reporters who probe at the sealed edges of her private life like ants running wildly over a capped sugar bowl. Berniece will insulate herself to protect her memories and preserve the sanctity of her relationship with Marilyn. She will read nothing more about Marilyn for seventeen years. With one exception. Because of her admiration for Arthur Miller, she will read his play *After the Fall*, which has for its female lead a woman inspired by Marilyn. The reading will make her ill and angry.

Meanwhile, Berniece searches for a rest home for Gladys in Florida while working out the preliminary steps for transferring her guardianship from Inez Melson. Gladys's desire for independence is an energizing force. At the age of sixty-three she succeeds in a spectacular escape from Rockhaven. She slides down a rope made of knotted uniforms, climbs a fence, and disappears into the San Fernando Valley. She walks all night, twelve miles, finally coming upon a church. Inside, she crawls behind a hot water heater and sleeps until she is discovered by the caretaker. The police deliver her back to Rockhaven, but not before her outing is immortalized by news and magazine photographers.

Gladys's bills begin to pile up at Rockhaven. There is no money to pay the bills submitted to probate court by Marilyn's creditors. No bequests can be granted.

Marilyn had arranged a system by which her income from her various assets, royalties, and so forth came to her in a set monthly salary. The arrangement would have prevented her from having to pay enormous amounts of tax all at once. So after her death money came in only very gradually. And as it did, large chunks had to be used for outstanding bills, storage fees, accountants' fees, taxes, and legal fees. For instance, reports at the end of the third year quoted

$958,138 owed in taxes and creditors' claims and earnings of only about eight hundred thousand dollars.

The terms of Marilyn's will could not be fulfilled because the money was nonexistent. After about three years, I simply put Marilyn's bequest to me out of my mind. But I had to take care of Mother's situation. Her only source of income was her Social Security check of $101.50, and her care at Rockhaven was three hundred dollars per month.

Finally, Mother was transferred to Camarillo State Hospital. After she attempted suicide, I took custody of her.

Supervision is essential. Sometimes Berniece's neighbors call her at work with reports of Gladys's accidents or misadventures. One neighbor smells a fire. She runs to the Miracle house and discovers that the electric iron has burned through the cover of the ironing board. Oblivious, Gladys is sitting in the living room reading Christian Science literature.

Gladys's present reality seems vague to her, her mind seething with dramas and events from the past. In the midst of a conversation, her mind will fly twenty or thirty years backward in time.

196

I think that being with me reminded her of the past. She passionately resented having a guardian. But when I got her a place in a new senior citizen project, she didn't like it either. She would leave every chance she got.

Marilyn's will is at last released from probate status in 1977. The trust fund for Gladys becomes active; one hundred thousand dollars in trust gives her the first annual check for five thousand dollars.

Accumulating enough money to begin executing the terms of Marilyn's will has taken the attorneys fifteen years. And Gladys is nowhere to be found. She has run off again.

Finally someone told me that Mother had returned and was living right here in town. Her drive for independence never faltered.

Even when she was bedridden in the nursing home, to the end of her days, she would jump the bed rails and make her way to the hall.

When Berniece retires, reporters change their tactics. The Miracles live in a secluded area with a fenced lot. Their house bears no address and the telephone is unlisted. Now Paris becomes a prime target.

Telephone calls to him at his office increase. They come from all directions—New York, Miami, California, even Europe. Often reporters chance a trip and then telephone locally.

Paris pretends to be divorced. He poses as a yardman, an electrician, a neighbor, and a deaf mute. He tells reporters that Berniece is in Europe or Jerusalem or has moved back to Flat Lick, Kentucky. Or he tells them she has died.

When Berniece eats lunch downtown occasionally, or goes shopping, she is likely to be interrupted by what she calls hit-and-run cameras. When confronted, she says simply, "We don't give stories." Friends are asked to call before coming to the house. Even the fence with its locked gate does not deter some agile climbers. Some get through the gates by posing as out-of-town policemen.

When Berniece's bulging correspondence files begin to outgrow the den, she tosses them into the trash and burns them. The barbeque pit serves as full-time secretary.

"I never wanted her to be an actress," declares Gladys. The subject of Marilyn springs into her conversation from nowhere, a subject on which she has been perpetually mute.

"You didn't want her to be an actress, but you named her after movie stars . . ." Berniece says.

"That is a lie! I did not. I named her after Norma Jeane Cohen in Louisville, Kentucky."

Mona Rae asks Gladys to tell about the grandmother who was a private eye but Gladys ignores the question. The tension caused by talk of Marilyn is excruciating.

"How did Marilyn die?" Gladys's unexpected question crashes into the silence.

"We think," gulps Berniece, "that she accidentally took an overdose of sleeping pills."

197

The white-haired lady's blue eyes widen into round hard marbles. "She shouldn't have been taking them!"

I don't know what to think about all the murder theories that have cropped up since Marilyn died. I think it was definitely not suicide. I have never believed that Marilyn deliberately took her own life. She was too excited about the things she was doing. Especially her new home. She had too many things that she enjoyed doing. She took sleeping pills, and she had taken too many in the past. I feel that she forgot how many she had taken, that it was an accident.

But certainly I would like to see a thorough investigation. I have never had the means. If I had, there are a lot of things I would have done. I wish I could have afforded the time away from home and family and the travel and the attorneys' fees.

After another difficult day with Gladys, Berniece begins to weep. "Why can't Mother act like a mother?" she breathes shakily. Her lower lip swells rapidly, her face turns pink, and her forefinger flies to steady her lips as she slowly shakes her head.

"You're tearing yourself apart," Mona Rae whispers intently to Berniece. "You have got to act in terms of what *is,* not what *should* be." She continues, her voice peppered with italics, "You can't continue hoping to acquire a mother. If anything, just the opposite has happened. Mamita has acquired a mother. You are her mother. And you are an orphan. Accept it."

Berniece remembers herself as a tiny girl on a bridge. The child sees the flaxen head of a stranger disappear over the crest of the bridge. The wind is blowing hard and cold, and it lashes the stinging ends of the child's hair into her eyes.

The wind ebbs into a hum . . . a whisper . . . notes that shimmer across the eardrum as the soft voice of another little girl carrying the words of a wistful grown-up Marilyn, marveling, "My ears are just like my father's. Just like them."

In Berniece's memory, the pressure of something more solid than the wind alights on the child's arm. A hand, bony but gentle, pats her arm, and clasps her hand. "Let's go home now," says Maggie's voice.

On this summer evening, Berniece hasn't the slightest doubt that Marilyn would look beautiful and regal—that she could certainly give her rivals like Elizabeth Taylor a run for their money. The thought brings the tips of a grin to the corners of her mouth.